Florence Tan's

Best Nyonya Recipes

Florence Tan's

Best Nyonya Recipes

Dedication

Dedicated with love to family and friends, especially to my mentor, Dato' Lim Bian Yam, who has taught me all that I know.

10 *Introduction*

Fish

14 Aromatic Steamed Fish 16 Fried Fish Balls 17 Spicy Chilli Fish
18 Fried Fish with Mango Salad 20 Otak-otak Belanga 22 Nyonya Fish Soup
24 Sweet and Sour Spicy Fish 26 Fish Pais 28 Crispy Sambal Lengkung

Chicken

30 Chicken Rumpah 32 Chilli Chicken 34 Petani Soup
36 Spicy Creamy Chicken 38 Spicy Sweet Dried Tamarind Chicken
40 Tempera Chicken 41 Spicy Chicken 42 Titik Chicken 44 Sek Chicken
46 Lor Chicken 48 Tofu with Minced Chicken 50 Chicken Sioh

Seafood

52 Fried Spicy Crabs 54 Fried Spicy Shrimp Paste Rice
55 Kerabu Udang and Timun (Prawn and Cucumber Salad) 56 Fried Squid à la Nyonya
58 Nyonya Prawn (Shrimp) Porridge 60 Spicy Prawn (Shrimp) Curry with Pineapple
62 Spicy Sweet and Sour Prawn (Shrimp) Curry 64 Sweet and Sour Squid
66 Special Fried Prawns (Shrimps) 68 Sambal Prawns (Shrimps)

Vegetables

70 Eggplants with Spicy Shrimp Dip   71 Spicy Tofu Soup   72 Chap Chye
74 Pineapple Patchree   76 Kangkong Masak Lemak   78 Kerabu Lady's Fingers
80 Mango Patchree   82 Mixed Vegetable Curry
84 Spicy Stuffed Bittergourd with Coconut Milk   86 Cencaluk Omelette

Desserts

88 Bubur Caca   90 Kuih Cara with Coconut Sauce   92 Kuih Genggang (Layered Cake)
94 Kuih Keledek Goreng (Fried Sweet Potato Balls)   96 Kuih Kosui
97 Bubur Pulut Hitam (Black Glutinous Rice Porridge with Dried Longans)
98 Kuih Talam   100 Pang Susi   102 Talam Keladi   104 Kuih Bongkong
106 Buah Melaka   108 Apam Manis

112 Basic Recipes

116 Cooking Tips

120 Glossary

127 Weights & Measures

Introduction

From a very tender age, much of my time was spent watching my mother cook. She was a very efficient and capable woman, cooking single-handedly all by herself, food for huge crowds of people. During Chinese New Year and other major festivals, my mother would labour for days churning out huge volumes of really tasty food to feed the large family gatherings. She was such an expert that despite cooking in big quantities, her food always turned out great. She would have huge pots of food cooking over charcoal stoves and would from time to time just open their lids and throw in seasonings almost without a blink. And the results were always right. It was the same with many of my aunties who were all great Nyonya cooks themselves. They would often come together to cook communally. Their meticulousness and their expert judgement honed by long years of cooking mentored by *bibiks* ensured excellent results, much to the delight of their immediate and extended families, who were the main consumers of their cooking. Such memorable feasts with so many different varieties of delicious food always appealed to me, and the colours of cooking became the great inspiration that eventually led me towards a much-loved culinary career.

Since my last book, **Secrets of Nyonya Cooking**, I have been most excited to share with you many more recipes on traditional Nyonya food that had not been possible to include there. This book is a natural extension of that desire. It carries recipes intrinsically different from and not found in my first book, but which I can assure you are equally authentic, unique and delicious, as they also use a myriad of herbs and spices. As before, the recipes include both savouries and mouth-watering desserts, all written with the same precision and care. Some of these are Otak-otak Belanga, Kerabu Udang and Timun, Talam Keladi and Kuih Bongkong.

Considering the huge repertoire of Nyonya recipes, I have by astute choice picked those famed as quintessentially Nyonya, and made the recipes easy to work with. I imagine both my mother and *bibik* would have been thrilled. My utmost thanks and appreciation go to Dato' Lim Bian Yam, who had not only taught me the finer tips on cooking, but also the great mysteries of the philosophy of life. He sincerely impressed upon me that having food is truly a wonderful blessing that ought to be revered and enjoyed. Till today, I still remember and practise his sentiment with great pleasure.

My heartfelt gratitude and warmest thanks also go to the many other persons who have extended their help to make this book a reality. They are my dearest sisters, nieces, relatives and friends. They helped kitchen-test, type and proofread my recipes, and were also willing guinea pigs who tried the recipes and provided valuable feedback. They unwaveringly supported me in many aspects of this culinary adventure.

Grateful thanks also go to the Marshall Cavendish team, my editors Audrey, Christine and Fiza, and to Pacino, the photographer and director who (once again) worked magic in producing the exceptionally beautiful pictures here.

My sincere wish for you all, my dear readers who love Nyonya food, is that this book will instill passion for reproducing authentic Nyonya dishes. May you savour and enjoy this collection of recipes. With this book I will have achieved my lifelong dream of leaving behind for posterity, a guide to secrets of truly delicious Nyonya food.

Florence Tan

Aromatic Steamed Fish

Serves 6

Red snapper or sea bass 500 g (1 lb 1 1/2 oz), scored whole or cut into pieces
Salt 1/2 tsp
Cornflour (cornstarch) 1/2 tsp
Ground white pepper 1/8 tsp
Cooking oil 1 Tbsp
Spring onions (scallions) 3 stalks

Finely Ground Ingredients
Torch ginger bud (*bunga kantan*) 1 stalk
Lemon grass 1 stalk
Red chillies 5
Kaffir lime leaves 3
Young ginger 2-cm (1-in) knob, peeled and finely sliced
Garlic 2 cloves, peeled and finely chopped

Seasoning
Salt 1/2 tsp
Sugar 2 1/4 Tbsp
Lime juice 2 1/4 Tbsp
Anchovy stock granules (*serbuk ikan bilis*) 1 1/4 tsp
Cornflour (cornstarch) 3/4 tsp

Garnishing
Sliced torch ginger bud (*bunga kantan*) 1 Tbsp
Red chilli 1 Tbsp, sliced
Kaffir lime leaves 1 Tbsp, sliced

1. Marinate red snapper or sea bass with salt, cornflour and pepper for 15 minutes.
2. Grease steaming tray with oil. Place spring onions on steaming tray.
3. Place marinated fish on top of spring onions.
4. Mix finely ground ingredients with seasoning. When the mixture is well combined, pour it over the fish.
5. Steam over high heat for 20 minutes or until cooked. Fish is cooked when the flesh turns from translucent to opaque.
6. Garnish with torch ginger bud, chilli and kaffir lime leaves. Serve hot.

NOTE
- The cooking time depends on the thickness of the fish meat. Thinner slabs of fish can be cooked between 10–15 minutes. Check doneness between 8–10 minutes and adjust the cooking time accordingly.

Fried Fish Balls

Serves 6

Salt 3/4 tsp
Iced water 5 Tbsp
Spanish mackerel 500 g (1 lb 1 1/2 oz)
Ground white pepper 1/4 tsp
Cornflour (cornstarch) 1 tsp
Cooking oil 500 ml (16 fl oz / 2 cups)
Chilli sauce (optional) to taste
Cucumber (optional) 10-cm (4-in) length, sliced

Garnishing
Salad leaves a handful

1. Dissolve salt in iced water.
2. Pound fish using a mortar and pestle or process in a blender. Gradually add salted iced water to fish and stir until it becomes a smooth paste.
3. Add pepper and cornflour. Using a metal spoon, stir in one direction for about 20 times. Divide fish paste into 2–3 portions.
4. Take each portion and hit it against the side of a mortar or bowl for about 30 times, until it becomes sticky and springy. Repeated hitting increases the elasticity of the fish paste and gives it a better texture.
5. Dab hands with oil. Scoop a handful of fish paste and roll it into a ball. Place on a well oiled plate to prevent sticking. Repeat until all the fish paste is used up.
6. Heat oil in a wok. When it is about 180°C (350°F), deep fry fish balls until light golden brown. Remove from heat and drain.
7. Garnish with salad leaves. Serve fish balls whole or sliced, with chilli sauce and cucumber if desired.

NOTE
- Do not over-fry fish balls or they will become chewy.

Spicy Chilli Fish

Serves 6

Senangin or red snapper 500 g (1 lb 1 1/2 oz), cut into fillets or smaller pieces
Salt 3/4 tsp
Cooking oil 100 ml (3 1/3 fl oz)
Kaffir lime leaves 6

Finely Ground Ingredients
Red chillies 400 g (14 oz)
Garlic 6 cloves, peeled

Seasoning
Salt 1 tsp
Anchovy stock granules (*serbuk ikan bilis*) 1 1/2 tsp

Garnishing
Red chilli 1, thinly sliced
Kaffir lime leaves 3

1. Marinate senangin or red snapper with salt for 10 minutes.
2. Heat oil in a wok. Fry fish until golden brown. Drain oil and place on a serving plate.
3. Prepare chilli paste. Fry finely ground ingredients in remaining oil until fragrant. Add seasoning and kaffir lime leaves. Cook for another 2–3 minutes, then pour over fried fish.
4. Garnish with red chilli and kaffir lime leaves. Serve immediately.

NOTE
- Any type of meaty fish can be used for this recipe. The fish may be fried whole or in smaller pieces.

Fried Fish with Mango Salad

Serves 6

Red snapper or sea bass fillet 400 g (14 oz), cut into fillets
Salt 1/2 tsp
Ground white pepper 1/4 tsp
Egg 1, slightly beaten
Cooking oil 600 ml (19 fl oz)
Plain (all-purpose) flour 60 g (2 oz)
Cornflour (cornstarch) 60 g (2 oz)

Mango Sauce
Maltose syrup 5 Tbsp
Honey 5 Tbsp
Light soy sauce 3 Tbsp
Kasturi lime juice 5 Tbsp
Mango cordial 5 Tbsp
Sugar 2 1/2 Tbsp
Salt 3/4 tsp
Cornflour (cornstarch) 1 tsp

Salad
Half-ripe mango about 150 g (5 1/3 oz), coarsely grated
Torch ginger bud (*bunga kantan*) 1 stalk, thinly sliced
Kaffir lime leaves 3, thinly sliced
Red chillies 2, thinly sliced
Bird's eye chillies 3, thinly sliced
Lemon grass 1 stalk, thinly sliced
Carrot 80 g (2 4/5 oz), peeled and finely grated
Shallots 7, about 70 g (2 1/2 oz), peeled and thinly sliced
Salt (optional) to taste
Sugar (optional) to taste

1. Marinate red snapper or sea bass fillet with salt, pepper and egg for 10 minutes.
2. Prepare mango sauce. In a saucepan, cook all ingredients for mango sauce over low heat until sugar dissolves. Remove from heat and set aside.
3. Heat oil in a wok. In the meantime, mix flour and cornflour. Coat marinated fish fillet with flour mixture. Deep-fry flour-coated fish fillet until golden brown. Drain oil and place fish on a serving plate.
4. Prepare salad. Except salt and sugar, combine all ingredients for salad in a bowl. Mix in 5 Tbsp mango sauce. Add salt and sugar if desired.
5. Pour salad over fried fish. Serve immediately.

NOTE
- Maltose syrup and honey tend to stick to measuring spoons. To prevent this, dip spoons in oil before measuring out maltose syrup and honey.
- Refrigerate remaining mango sauce for future use. If chilled, it can be kept for up to 5 days.

Otak-otak Belanga

Serves 6

Spanish mackerel fillet 650 g (1 lb 7 oz)
Salt 1 tsp
Cornflour (cornstarch) 4 tsp
Iced water 180 ml (6 fl oz / ¾ cup)
Ground white pepper ¼ tsp
Cooking oil 180 ml (6 fl oz / ¾ cup)
Water 450 ml (15 fl oz)
Kaffir lime leaves 5
Young turmeric leaves 3, cut into 5-cm (2-in) lengths
Thick coconut milk (page 116) 250 ml (8 fl oz / 1 cup)

Finely Ground Ingredients

Dried red chillies 20, deseeded, soaked in boiling water in a covered bowl for 20 minutes until soft
Red chillies 6
Galangal 3-cm (1¼-in) knob, peeled
Fresh turmeric 3.5-cm (1½-in) knob, peeled
Candlenuts (*buah keras*) 6
Shrimp paste (*belacan*) granules 2 tsp
Coriander (cilantro) powder 1½ tsp
Shallots 25, about 250 g (9 oz), peeled
Lemon grass 4 stalks

Seasoning

Salt 1 tsp
Sugar 3 tsp
Anchovy stock granules (*serbuk ikan bilis*) 1 tsp

Garnishing

Young turmeric leaves 1 tsp, thinly sliced

NOTE

- Shrimp paste (*belacan*) granules may be substituted with shrimp paste (*belacan*). For every 1 tsp of shrimp paste granules, substitute with a small amount of belacan paste, the size of a 1.5–2.5-cm (¾–1-in) lump. Adjust according to taste.

- To test if fish paste is springy, tap in quick succession, and dents should not remain on the paste.

- The sauce will thicken when cooled. Add required amount of hot water to dilute the sauce if reheating the dish.

20 Florence Tan's Best Nyonya Recipes

1. Process fish fillet in a blender with salt and cornflour, adding iced water gradually. Blend until a smooth paste forms and empty into a big bowl.
2. Stir paste in one direction until well-mixed and very sticky. Divide into 2 portions. Take 1 portion and repeatedly hit it against the bowl about 20 times until springy. Repeat for the other portion.
3. Dab hands with oil. Roll 50–60 g (1 $^{3}/_{5}$–2 oz) of paste into a ball. Flatten into a 6-mm ($^{1}/_{4}$-in) thick rectangle. Place fish cake onto a lightly-greased plate to prevent sticking. Repeat process with wet hands until all the paste has been used.
4. Heat oil in a wok. Fry finely ground ingredients until fragrant. Add water, seasoning, kaffir lime leaves and turmeric leaves. When boiling, reduce heat and simmer for 7 minutes.
5. Increase heat and add fish cakes. Cook for 6 minutes. Stir in coconut milk. When it comes to a boil, remove from heat.
6. Garnish with turmeric leaves and serve immediately.

Fish 21

Nyonya Fish Soup

Serves 6

Water 1.6 litres (54 fl oz / 6¾ cups)
Ginger 1.5-cm (¾-in) knob, peeled and thinly sliced
Big onions 2, peeled and quartered
Red snapper, senangin or wolf herring 500 g (1 lb 1½ oz), cut into pieces
Red chilli 1, deseeded and cut into triangles

Seasoning
Salt 1 tsp
Ground white pepper ¼ tsp
Anchovy stock granules (*serbuk ikan bilis*) ¾ tsp

Dipping sauce
Light soy sauce 3 Tbsp
Kasturi lime juice 1½ tsp
Red chilli 1, sliced

Garnishing
Coriander (cilantro) leaves 1 sprig
Chopped spring onion 1 tsp

1. In a saucepan, bring water and ginger slices to a boil. Add big onions and cook for another 5 minutes.
2. Add seasoning and fish. Bring to a boil and add chilli. When fish is cooked, remove from heat.
3. Garnish with coriander leaves and spring onion. Serve with dipping sauce.

NOTE
- If using wolf herring, it is easier to cut it into big pieces.
- To cut a fresh chilli into triangles, halve it first. Taking one half, diagonally slit it from the bottom end to the top. Diagonally slit the same half again such that the two slits form a cross. Repeat for the other half of the chilli.

Florence Tan's Best Nyonya Recipes

Sweet and Sour Spicy Fish

Serves 6-8

Red snapper 800 g (1 3/4 oz), cut into pieces

Salt 3/4 tsp

Ground white pepper 1/4 tsp

Spring onions (scallions) 4 stalks

Cooking oil 125 ml (4 fl oz / 1/2 cup)

Tamarind juice extracted from 45 g (1 1/2 oz) tamarind pulp and 500 ml (16 fl oz / 2 cups) water

Fresh pineapple slices 100 g (3 1/2 oz), cut into triangles

Polygonum (*kesum*) leaves 1 sprig

Torch ginger bud (*bunga kantan*) 1 stalk

Eggplant (aubergine/brinjal) 100 g (3 1/2 oz), cut into 3.5-cm (1 1/2-in) lengths

Big onion 1, peeled and quartered

Lady's fingers (okra) or long beans 50 g (1 2/3 oz), cut into 5-cm (2-in) lengths

Tomato 1, cut into wedges

Green chilli 1, deseeded and cut into triangles (see Note on page 22.)

Finely Ground Ingredients

Dried red chillies 20, deseeded, soaked in boiling water in a covered bowl for 20 minutes until soft

Shallots 20, about 200 g (7 oz), peeled

Garlic 3 cloves, peeled

Fresh turmeric 2.5-cm (1-in) knob, peeled

Galangal 1.5-cm (3/4-in) knob, peeled

Lemon grass 3 stalks

Shrimp paste (*belacan*) granules 1 tsp (See Note on page 20.)

Candlenuts (*buah keras*) 4

Seasoning

Salt 1 1/4 tsp

Anchovy granules 3/4 tsp

Sugar 2 1/2 Tbsp

1. Marinate red snapper with salt and pepper for 5 minutes.
2. Place spring onions on steaming tray.
3. Place marinated fish on top of spring onions and steam over high heat for 20–25 minutes.
4. Meanwhile, heat oil in a wok, fry finely ground ingredients until fragrant. Pour in tamarind juice and bring to a boil.
5. Over medium-low heat, add pineapple, polygonum leaves, torch ginger bud and eggplant. Simmer for $2^{1}/_{2}$ minutes.
6. Add seasoning, big onion, lady's fingers, tomato and green chilli. Simmer for a further $2^{1}/_{2}$ minutes or until vegetables are tender. Set spicy mixture aside.
7. When fish is done, discard water and transfer to a serving plate. Pour spicy mixture over fish and serve hot.

Fish Pais

Makes 10–15 parcels

Spanish mackerel 600 g (1 lb 5 2/5 oz), cut into 3-cm (1 1/4-in) steaks
Salt 3/4 tsp
Ground white pepper 1/4 tsp
Thinly sliced kaffir lime leaves 2 Tbsp
Banana leaves 10–15, each 18 x 22 cm (7 x 9 in), washed, scalded and wiped dry
Banana leaves 10–15, each 4 x 15 cm (1 3/4 x 6 in), washed, scalded and wiped dry
Strong toothpicks 10–15

Finely Ground Ingredients
Red chillies 200 g (7 oz)
Shallots 36, about 360 g (12 3/4 oz), peeled
Shrimp paste (*belacan*) granules 1 1/2 tsp (See Note on page 20.)

Seasoning
Anchovy stock granules (*serbuk ikan bilis*) 1 Tbsp
Salt 3/4 tsp
Sugar 4 tsp

Garnishing
Thinly sliced kaffir lime leaves 1 Tbsp

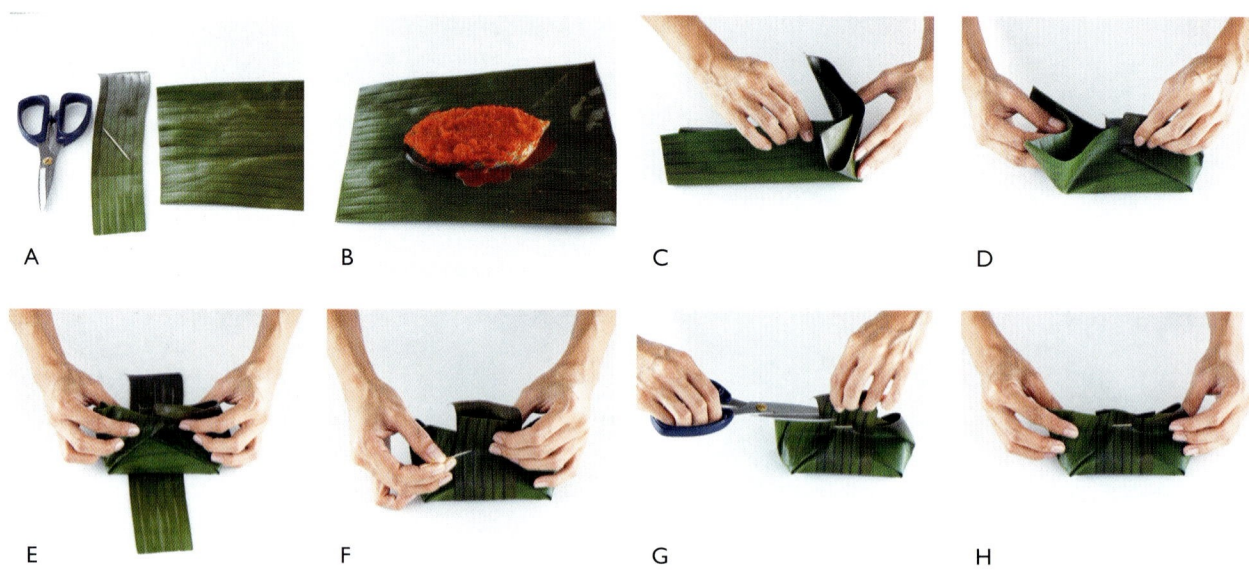

A B C D
E F G H

26 *Florence Tan's Best Nyonya Recipes*

1. Marinate Spanish mackerel with salt and pepper for 10 minutes.
2. Mix kaffir lime leaves with finely ground ingredients, then mix in seasoning. Mix until mixture is well combined.
3. Set half a portion of mixture aside, then spread it over fish steaks, making sure they are well-coated.
4. Arrange 1–2 fish steaks on the centre of a 18- x 22-cm (7- x 9-in) banana leaf. From the half portion mixture that was set aside earlier, spread 2–4 Tbsp of mixture on top of fish steaks. Bring the ends of the banana leaf together and wrap like you would for Kuih Bongkong (page 104). See facing page for method of wrapping.
5. Use a 4- x 15-cm (1 3/4- x 6-in) banana leaf to wrap around the folded bundle before fastening with a toothpick. Using scissors, trim off excess banana leaf.
6. Repeat steps 4–5 until all fish steaks have been used.
7. Place wrapped fish steaks on steaming tray. Steam for 20–25 minutes.
8. Garnish with kaffir lime leaves and serve immediately.

Fish

Crispy Sambal Lengkung

Makes about 200 g (7 oz)

Spanish mackerel 600 g (1 lb 5²/₅ oz), cut into 7.5-cm (3-in) lengths
Tamarind juice extracted from 20 g (²/₃ oz) tamarind pulp and 300 ml (10 fl oz / 1¼ cup) water
Lemon grass 2 stalks, bruised
Polygonum (*kesum*) leaves 2 sprigs
Torch ginger bud (*bunga kantan*) 1 stalk
Galangal 2-cm (³/₄-in) knob, peeled
Sugar 4 Tbsp (to be added only at step 5)

Finely Ground Ingredients
Dried red chillies 10, deseeded, soaked in boiling water in a covered bowl for 20 minutes until soft
Shallots 7, about 70 g (2½ oz), peeled
Fresh turmeric 2.5-cm (1-in) knob, peeled

Seasoning
Salt 1¼ tsp
Sugar 1½ tsp

1. Heat all ingredients with finely ground ingredients and seasoning in a deep saucepan. Bring to a boil. Lower heat and cook until gravy becomes dry.
2. Remove from heat and leave to cool. Remove lemon grass, polygonum leaves, torch ginger bud and galangal.
3. De-bone fish and break it into flakes. Process fish flakes in a blender until finely blended.
4. Heat a non-stick pan and cook blended fish over medium heat until almost dry, stirring constantly.
5. Reduce heat to very low and keep frying until fish granules are crispy. Add 4 Tbsp sugar and stir for half a minute.
6. Remove from heat and allow to cool.
7. Serve with toasted bread. Store remainder in an airtight bottle.

NOTE
- It is easier to process the fish in a blender rather than mash it with your hands.
- Crispy sambal lengkung can be kept in the refrigerator for up to 3 weeks.

Chicken Rumpah

The recipe for this scrumptious dish was from my mentor, Dato' Lim Bian Yam.

Serves 7

Cooking oil 100 ml (3 1/3 fl oz)

Big onions 2, peeled and cut into 1.25-cm (1/2-in) wedges

Chicken fillet 500 g (1 lb 1 1/2 oz), cut into 2- × 5-cm (1- × 2-in) slices

Thick coconut milk (page 116) 120 ml (3 3/4 fl oz)

Thinly sliced kaffir lime leaves 2 Tbsp

Finely Ground Ingredients

Fresh red chillies 6, seeded

Dried red chillies 5, seeded, soaked in boiling water in a covered bowl for 20 minutes until soft

Shallots 12, about 120 g (4 1/3 oz), peeled

Shrimp paste (*belacan*) granules 1 tsp (See Note on page 20.)

Candlenuts (*buah keras*) 5

Seasoning

Sugar 1 Tbsp

Salt 1 tsp

Chicken stock granules 1/4 tsp

Garnishing

Thinly sliced kaffir lime leaves 1 Tbsp

1. Heat 1 1/2 Tbsp oil in a wok. Fry onion wedges for a few minutes until crisp. Remove from heat and set aside.
2. Fry finely ground ingredients in remaining oil until fragrant. Add chicken slices and fry for 4 minutes. Add coconut milk, kaffir lime leaves and seasoning.
3. Lower heat and simmer until chicken is cooked and the sauce thick and semi-dry.
4. Add fried onions and cook for 1–2 minutes more.
5. Garnish with kaffir lime leaves and serve immediately.

Chilli Chicken

Serves 6

Cooking oil 180 ml (6 fl oz / ¾ cup)

Chicken 1 kg (2 lb 3 oz), cut into pieces

Water 500 ml (16 fl oz / 2 cups)

Kaffir lime leaves 6

Kasturi lime juice 2 Tbsp

Finely Ground Ingredients

Red chillies 7

Dried red chillies 30, deseeded, soaked in boiling water in a covered bowl for 20 minutes until soft

Shallots 20, about 200 g (7 oz), peeled

Candlenuts (*buah keras*) 6

Seasoning

Light soy sauce 1 Tbsp

Salt 1 tsp

Chicken stock granules 1½ tsp

Sugar 2 tsp

1. Heat oil in a wok. Fry finely ground ingredients until fragrant.
2. Add chicken and fry for 5 minutes. Pour in water and bring to a boil.
3. Reduce heat and add kaffir lime leaves. Allow to simmer for 10–15 minutes. Add seasoning.
4. When chicken is tender, stir in lime juice.
5. Remove from heat and serve immediately.

Petani Soup

Serves 10

Chicken curry powder 2 Tbsp
Water 2 Tbsp
Macaroni 100 g (3 1/2 oz)
Cooking oil 3 Tbsp
Lemon grass 2 stalks, bruised
Chicken fillet 300 g (10 1/2 oz), cut into 1/2-cm cubes
Button mushrooms 180 g (6 1/3 oz), sliced
Chicken stock (page 113) 2.5 litres (80 fl oz / 10 cups)
Green peas 200 g (7 oz)

Finely Ground Ingredients

Dried red chillies 3, seeded, soaked in boiling water in a covered bowl for 20 minutes until soft
Shrimp paste (*belacan*) granules 1 tsp (See Note on page 20.)
Shallots 7, about 70 g (2 1/2 oz), peeled

Seasoning

Salt 1 1/4 tsp
Sugar 1 1/2 tsp
Chicken stock granules 1 1/2 tsp

Garnishing

Croutons 30 g (1 oz)
Shallot crisps (page 112) 15 g (1/2 oz)

1. Prepare curry paste. Mix chicken curry powder with water. Set aside for at least 4 hours so that the paste will be well-blended and not burn easily during cooking.
2. Prepare macaroni according to package instructions.
3. Heat oil in a wok. Fry finely ground ingredients until fragrant. Stir in curry paste and lemon grass.
4. Add chicken and cook until it changes colour. Add mushrooms and fry for 3 minutes.
5. Pour in chicken stock and bring to a boil. Lower heat and allow to simmer for 7 minutes. Add seasoning.
6. Add green peas. Remove from heat.
7. Scoop a few Tbsp macaroni into each serving bowl. Ladle soup over macaroni.
8. Garnish with croutons and shallot crisps before serving.

NOTE
- To prepare your own croutons, cut fresh bread into cubes and bake them in the oven or deep-fry until golden brown. Store in airtight tins to preserve their crispness.

Spicy Creamy Chicken

Serves 8

Cooking oil 150 ml (5 fl oz)

Chicken 1 kg (2 lb 3 oz), cut into pieces

Water 800 ml (27 fl oz)

Potatoes 500 g (1 lb 1½ oz), peeled and quartered

Asam gelugur 1 slice

Kaffir lime leaves 2

Thick coconut milk (page 116) 200 ml (6¾ fl oz)

Finely Ground Ingredients

Dried red chillies 20, deseeded, soaked in boiling water in a covered bowl for 20 minutes until soft

Red chillies 3

Shallots 15, about 150 g (5⅓ oz), peeled

Garlic 3 cloves, peeled

Lemon grass 3 stalks

Galangal 1.7-cm (¾-in) knob, peeled

Fresh turmeric 2-cm (1-in) knob, peeled

Candlenuts (*buah keras*) 4

Shrimp paste (*belacan*) granules 2 tsp (See Note on page 20.)

Seasoning

Salt 2 tsp

Chicken stock granules 2 tsp

Sugar 1½ Tbsp

Garnishing

Kaffir lime leaves 2

Coriander (cilantro) leaves 1 sprig

1. Heat oil in a wok. Fry finely ground ingredients until fragrant.
2. Add chicken and fry for 5 minutes. Pour in water and bring to a boil.
3. Add potatoes, asam gelugur, kaffir lime leaves and seasoning. Lower heat and simmer until chicken is tender and potatoes are soft.
4. Add coconut milk and stir constantly to prevent curdling. When it has boiled for 2 minutes, remove from heat.
5. Garnish with kaffir lime leaves and coriander leaves. Serve immediately.

Chicken 37

Spicy Sweet Dried Tamarind Chicken

Serves 6

Cooking oil 140 ml (4 3/4 fl oz)

Lemon grass 2, bruised

Tamarind juice extracted from 50 g (1 2/3 oz) tamarind pulp and 600 ml (19 fl oz) water

Chicken 1 kg (2 lb 3 oz), cut into pieces

Torch ginger bud (*bunga kantan*) 1 stalk

Finely Ground Ingredients

Shallots 12, about 120 g (4 1/3 oz), peeled

Garlic 3 cloves, peeled

Dried red chillies, 10, deseeded, soaked in boiling water in a covered bowl for 20 minutes until soft

Red chillies 4

Candlenuts (*buah keras*) 6

Seasoning

Salt 1 tsp

Chicken stock granules 1 tsp

Sugar 3 Tbsp

1. Heat oil in a wok. Fry finely ground ingredients and lemon grass until fragrant.
2. Add chicken and fry for 2 minutes. Add tamarind juice, torch ginger bud and seasoning.
3. Cook until chicken is tender. The gravy should be very thick and coats the chicken meat.
4. Serve immediately with rice.

Chicken 39

Tempera Chicken

Serves 6

Cooking oil 4 Tbsp
Garlic 8 cloves, peeled and minced
Big onions 300–400 g (10 1/2–14 oz), peeled, thinly sliced
Red chillies 3, thinly sliced
Chicken 1 kg (2 lb 3 oz), cut into pieces
Chicken stock (page 113) 500 ml (16 fl oz / 2 cups)
Vinegar 2 Tbsp

Seasoning

Dark soy sauce 1 Tbsp
Light soy sauce 1 Tbsp
Sugar 1 Tbsp
Chicken stock granules 1 tsp
Salt 3/4 tsp

Garnishing

Thinly sliced red chilli 1 tsp
Coriander (cilantro) leaves 1 sprig

1. Heat oil in a wok. Fry garlic until fragrant. Add big onions and red chillies. Fry for 4 minutes and dish out half portion of the mixture. Set aside.
2. Add chicken to saucepan and fry for 3 minutes. Add chicken stock and seasoning. Cook until chicken is tender and the gravy is thick. Stir in half portion mixture that was set aside. Add vinegar and cook for 2 minutes.
3. Dish out and garnish with red chilli and coriander. Serve immediately.

Spicy Chicken

Serves 6

Cooking oil 100 ml (3 1/3 fl oz)
Chicken 1 kg (2 lb 3 oz), cut into pieces
Lemon grass 4, bruised
Water 400 ml (13 1/2 fl oz)
Kaffir lime leaves 4

Finely Ground Ingredients

Dried red chillies 25, deseeded, soaked in boiling water in a covered bowl for 20 minutes until soft
Shallots 15, about 150 g (5 1/3 oz), peeled
Garlic 4 cloves, peeled
Candlenuts (*buah keras*) 7
Shrimp paste (*belacan*) **granules** 1 1/2 tsp (See Note on page 20.)

Seasoning

Salt 1 tsp
Chicken stock granules 1 1/2 tsp
Sugar 2 Tbsp

1. Heat oil in a wok. Fry finely ground ingredients until fragrant.
2. Stir in chicken and lemon grass. Cook for a few minutes.
3. Pour in water and bring to a boil. Add kaffir lime leaves and seasoning.
4. Lower heat and simmer until chicken is tender and sauce is very thick.
5. Remove from heat and serve with rice.

Titik Chicken

Serves 6

Lemon grass 4 stalks, bruised and cut into 9-cm (3 1/2-in) lengths
Water 1.1 litres (37 fl oz)
Chicken 1 kg (2 lb 3 oz), cut into pieces
Kaffir lime leaves 6

Finely Ground Ingredients

Dried red chillies 25, seeded, soaked in boiling water in a covered bowl for 20 minutes until soft
Shallots 18, about 180 g (6 1/3 oz), peeled
Garlic 4 cloves, peeled
Candlenuts (*buah keras*) 8
Shrimp paste (*belacan*) granules, 1 1/2 tsp (See Note on page 20.)

Seasoning

Salt 1 1/4 tsp
Chicken stock granules 1 1/2 tsp
Sugar 2 Tbsp

Garnishing

Shredded coriander (cilantro) leaves 1 tsp

1. Place finely ground ingredients, lemon grass and water in a wok. Bring to a boil. Lower heat and allow to simmer for 10 minutes.
2. Add chicken, kaffir lime leaves and seasoning.
3. Cook until chicken is tender, and gravy is thick and of the same consistency as *rendang*.
4. Garnish with coriander leaves and serve immediately.

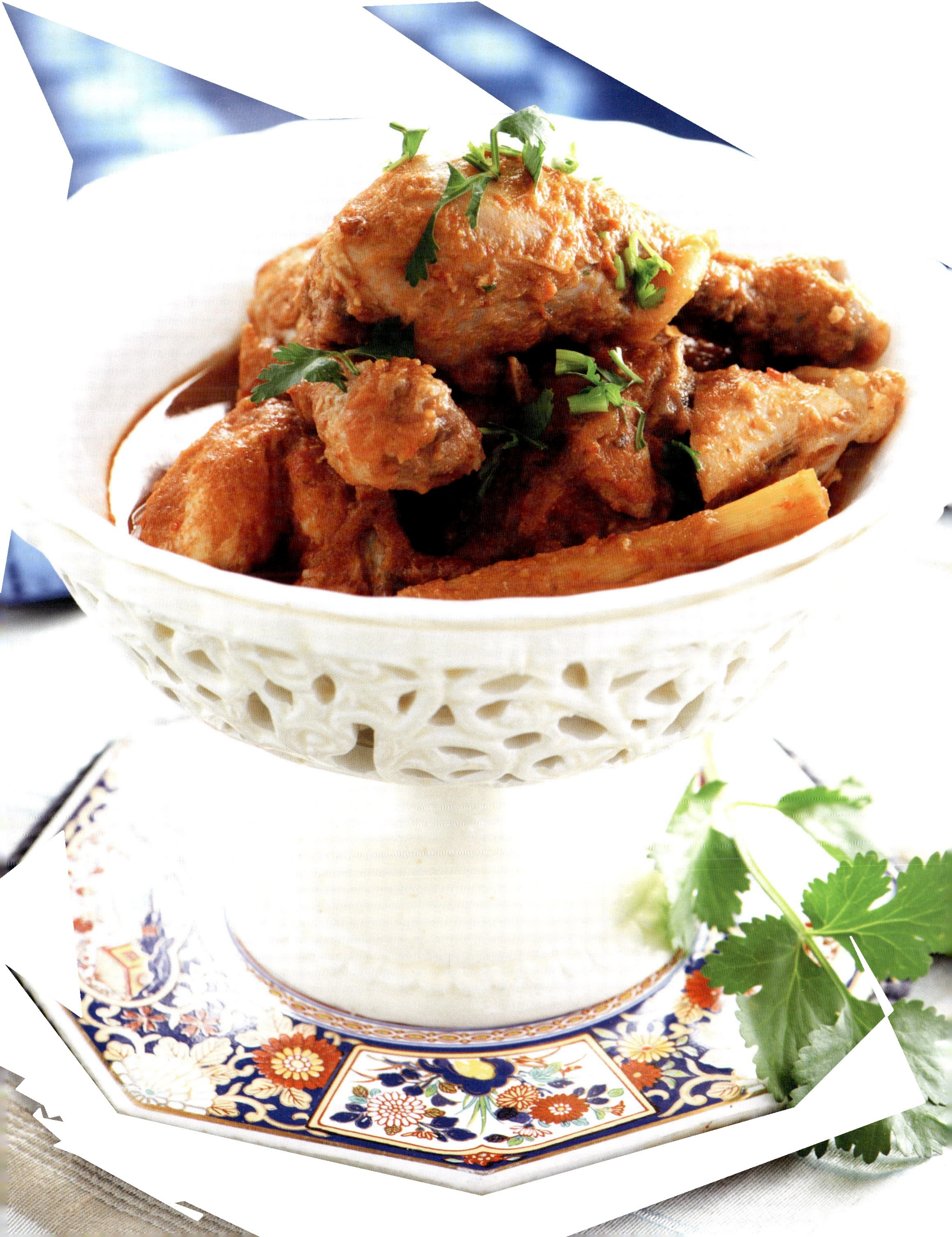

Sek Chicken

Serves 8

Chicken 1.5 kg (3 lb 4½ oz), cut into pieces
Light soy sauce 2 Tbsp
Sugar 1 Tbsp
Fried bean curd puffs (*tau pok*) 16 pieces
Cooking oil 150 ml (5 fl oz)
Galangal 1.5–2-cm (¾–1-in) knob, peeled and sliced into five 3-mm (⅛-in) slices
Shallots 20, about 200 g (7 oz), peeled and finely blended
Water 1 litre (32 fl oz / 4 cups)
Hard boiled eggs 6, shelled and halved

Spices

Cinnamon stick 1, 5-cm (2-in) length
Cloves 5
Star anise 2

Seasoning

Dark soy sauce 4½ Tbsp
Salt 1½ tsp
Sugar 4 Tbsp
Light soy sauce 1½ Tbsp
Ground white pepper ¼ tsp

Chilli Sauce

Fresh red chillies 120 g (4⅓ oz), finely blended
Garlic 5 cloves, peeled and finely blended
Salt 1½ tsp
Kasturi lime juice 3 Tbsp
Sugar 6½ Tbsp
Ground peanuts 100 g (3½ oz), toasted and finely pounded

Garnishing

Salad leaves a handful

1. Marinate chicken with light soy sauce and sugar for 1 hour.
2. Blanch fried bean curd puffs in boiling water for 3 minutes. Drain and set aside to cool. Squeeze dry of water and cut into halves.
3. Heat oil in a wok. Fry spices for half a minute. Add galangal and shallots. Fry until fragrant.
4. Add marinated chicken and fry for 3 minutes. Add water and seasoning. Bring to a boil.
5. Lower heat and simmer for 20 minutes.
6. Meanwhile, combine all ingredients for chilli sauce.
7. Scoop 250 ml (8 fl oz / 1 cup) gravy out of the wok into a bowl. Mix with chilli sauce. Set spicy sauce aside.
8. Add fried bean curd puffs and hard boiled eggs into the wok. Continue cooking until chicken is tender and gravy is thick.
9. Remove from heat and transfer chicken pieces onto a serving dish first, then pour gravy from saucepan over chicken.
10. Garnish with salad leaves and serve with spicy sauce.

Lor Chicken

Serves 6

Cooking oil 4 Tbsp
Sugar 4 1/2 Tbsp
Garlic 5 cloves, peeled
Cinnamon stick 1, 5-cm (2-in) length
Star anise 1
Cloves 5
Light soy sauce 2 1/2 Tbsp
Dark soy sauce 2 Tbsp
Five-spice powder 1 tsp
Water 400 ml (13 1/2 fl oz)
Chicken 1 kg (2 lb 3 oz), cut into pieces
Chilli sauce (optional) to taste

Garnishing
Chilli flakes 1 tsp
Spring onion 1 stalk

1. Heat oil in a wok over low heat. Without stirring, allow sugar to caramelise until slightly golden brown.
2. Stir in garlic, cinnamon stick, star anise and cloves. Fry for half a minute.
3. Add light soy sauce, dark soy sauce and five-spice powder. Cook for half a minute. Pour in water slowly and bring to a boil.
4. Add chicken. Cook over medium heat until chicken is tender and sauce becomes a thick syrup.
5. Garnish with chilli flakes and spring onion. Serve with chilli sauce if desired.

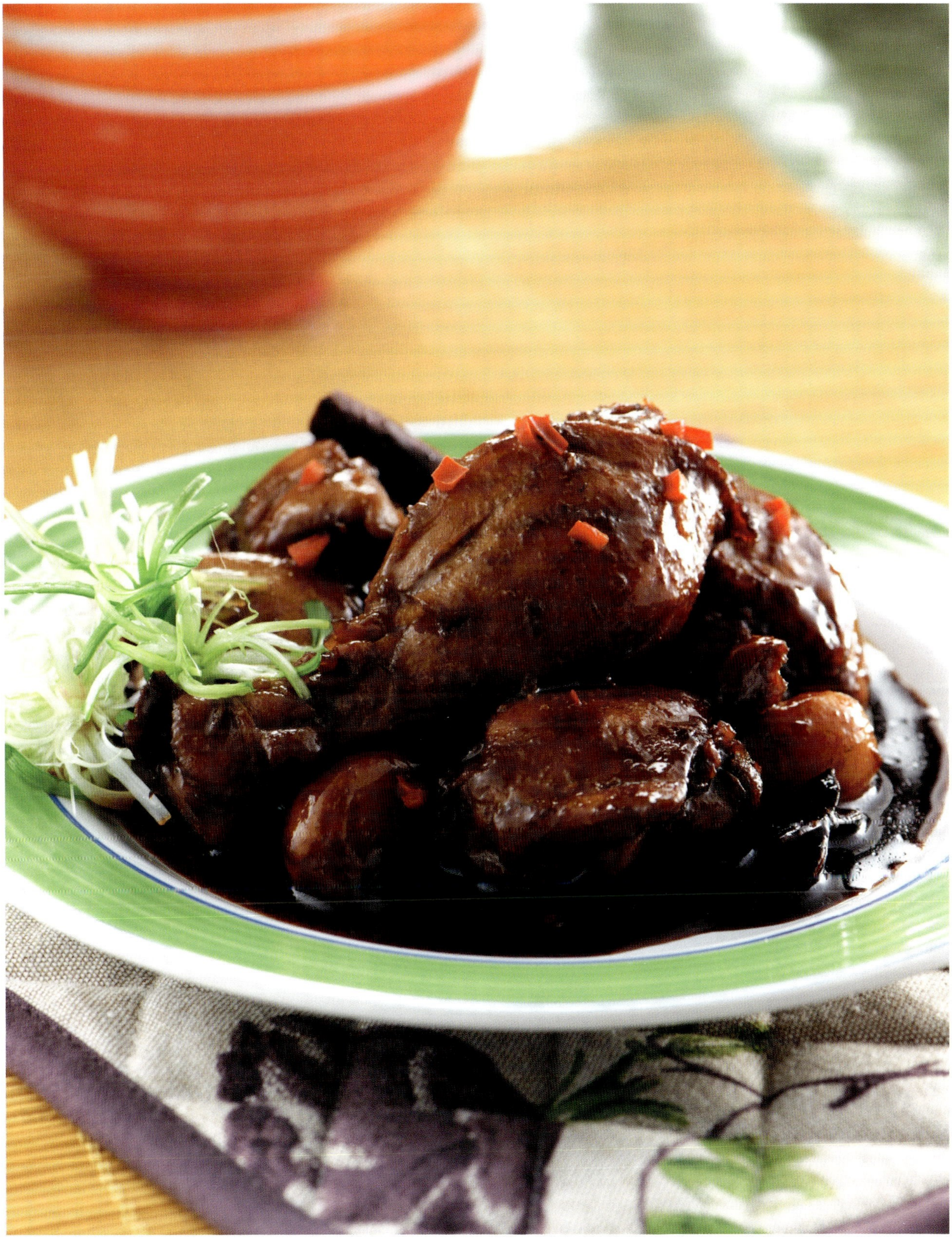

Tofu with Minced Chicken

Serves 6

Silken tofu 2 boxes, 300 g (10 1/2 oz) each
Cooking oil 3 Tbsp
Chopped garlic 1 Tbsp
Minced chicken 100 g (3 1/2 oz)
Chicken stock (page 113) 200 ml (6 3/4 fl oz)
Cornflour (cornstarch) 1/2 tsp, mixed with 1 tsp water

Seasoning
Oyster sauce 2 Tbsp
Light soy sauce 1 Tbsp
Dark soy sauce 1/4 tsp
Ground white pepper 1/4 tsp
Sugar 1/2 tsp

Garnishing
Shallots crisps (page 112) 1 Tbsp
Chopped spring onion (scallion) 2 Tbsp
Red chilli 1, finely sliced

1. Transfer tofu to a heat-proof dish. Steam tofu at high heat for 5 minutes. Remove from heat and drain off water.
2. Heat oil in a wok. Fry garlic until fragrant. Add minced chicken and fry until it changes colour.
3. Pour in chicken stock and bring to a boil. Add seasoning.
4. Thicken gravy with cornflour mixture. Bring to a boil.
5. Remove from heat. Transfer tofu to a serving dish first, then pour gravy over tofu.
6. Garnish with shallot crisps, spring onion and chilli. Serve hot.

Chicken 49

Chicken Sioh

Serves 6

Coriander (cilantro) powder 2½ Tbsp
Chicken 1 kg (2 lb 3 oz), cut into bite-sized pieces
Ground white pepper ¼ tsp
Shallots 20, about 200 g (7 oz), finely blended
Tamarind juice extracted from 40 g (1⅓ oz) tamarind pulp and 600 ml (19 fl oz) water

Seasoning

Light soy sauce 2 Tbsp
Dark soy sauce 1 Tbsp
Salt ¾ tsp
Sugar 3½ Tbsp

Garnishing

Salad leaves a handful
Red chilli 1, thinly sliced

1. Pan fry coriander powder until fragrant. Remove from heat and set aside.
2. Mix all ingredients with seasoning and pan-fried coriander powder in a saucepan and bring to a boil.
3. Lower heat to medium and simmer until chicken is tender and the sauce is thick. Remove from heat.
4. Garnish with salad leaves and red chilli. Serve with rice.

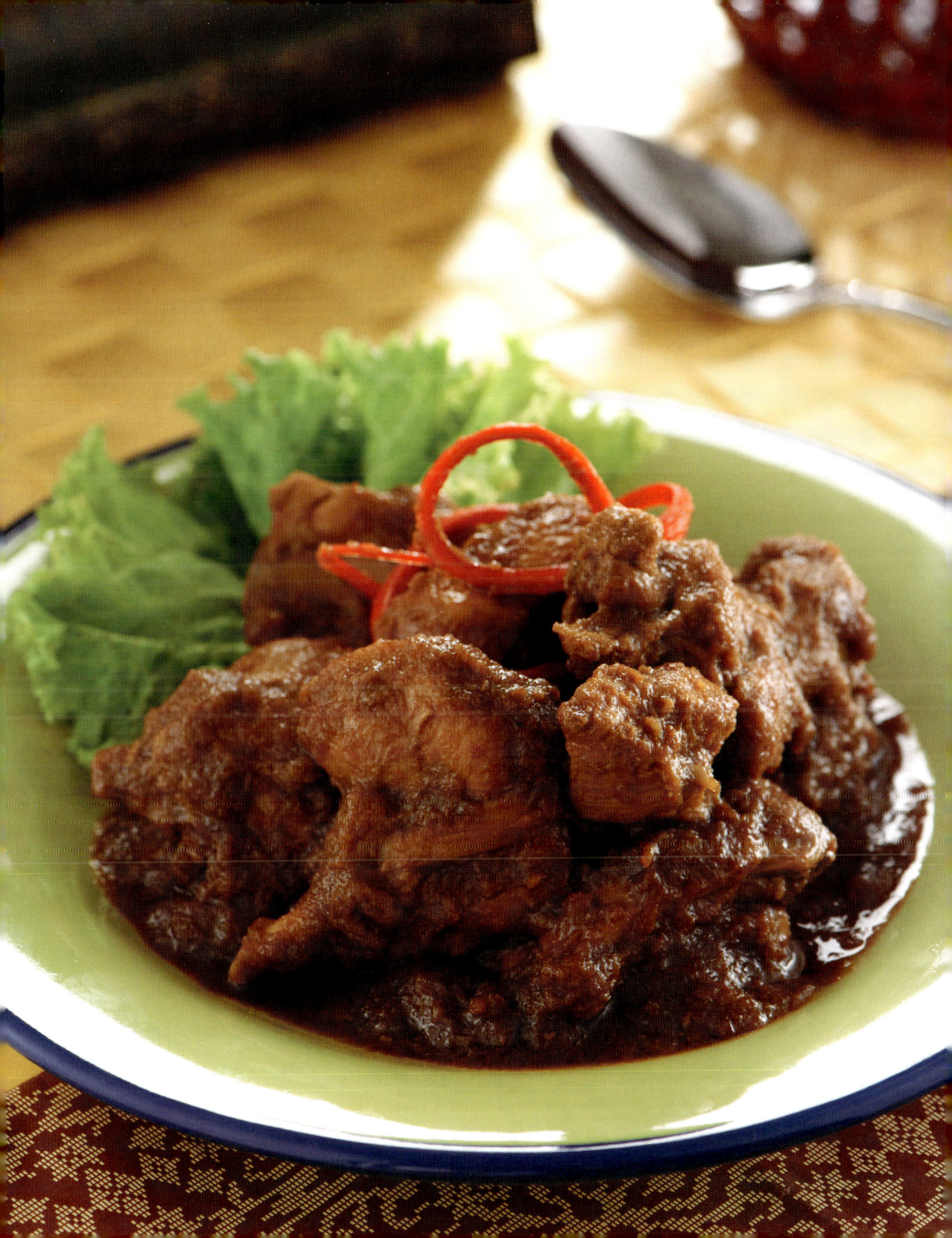

Fried Spicy Crabs

Serves 2-4

Dried shrimps 30 g (1 oz)
Cooking oil 500 ml (16 fl oz / 2 cups)
Crabs 1.5 kg (3 lb 4½ oz), cleaned and cut into pieces
Curry leaves 3 sprigs
Minced garlic 1½ Tbsp
Fermented soy bean paste (*tau cheo*) 1 Tbsp
Lemon grass 3 stalks, bruised
Bird's eye chillies 10, thinly sliced
Curry paste 2 Tbsp curry powder mixed with 2½ Tbsp water
Water 300 ml (10 fl oz / 1¼ cups)

Seasoning

Anchovy stock granules (*serbuk ikan bilis*) 1 tsp
Light soy sauce 1 Tbsp
Sugar 1½ Tbsp or to taste
Salt to taste

Garnishing

Red chilli 1, sliced

1. Rinse dried shrimps, then soak for 5 minutes. Process in a blender until finely blended. Set aside.
2. Heat oil in a wok. Deep-fry crabs until three-quarters cooked. Remove from heat and set aside.
3. Leave 6 Tbsp oil in wok to fry curry leaves and garlic until fragrant. Stir in fermented bean paste and fry over low heat until fragrant.
4. Add blended dried shrimps and fry until fragrant. Add lemon grass and bird's eye chillies.
5. Add curry paste and cook until oil surfaces to the top. Add seasoning and water. Bring to a boil, then lower heat and allow to simmer for 2–3 minutes.
6. Return crabs to the wok. Increase heat and cook until gravy is thick and coats the crab.
7. Dish out on a serving plate and garnish with red chilli slices. Serve hot.

Seafood 53

Fried Spicy Shrimp Paste Rice

Rice Serves 7

Dried shrimps 70 g (2½ oz)
Cooking oil 150 ml (5 fl oz)
Spicy shrimp paste (*sambal belacan*) (page 112) 4 Tbsp
Prawns (shrimps) 400 g (14 oz), cleaned, shelled and deveined
Eggs 2
Cooked rice 1 kg (2 lb 3 oz), fluffed up
Anchovy stock granules (*serbuk ikan bilis*) ½ tsp

Seasoning
Salt (optional) to taste

Garnishing
Egg omelette thinly sliced
Spring onion (scallion) 1 stalk, sliced into thin strips
Red chillies 2, sliced
Shallot crisps (page 112) 2 Tbsp

1. Rinse dried shrimps, then soak for 7 minutes. Process in a blender until finely blended. Set aside.
2. Heat oil in a non-stick pan. Fry blended dried shrimps until fragrant. Add spicy shrimp paste and fry until fragrant.
3. Add prawns. Fry prawns until they change colour.
4. Break eggs over mixture and cook until half set. Add rice to cover eggs for one minute before stirring. Add anchovy stock granules, and salt if using. Fry over high heat for 3–5 minutes.
5. Garnish with egg omelette, spring onion, red chillies and shallot crisps. Serve immediately.

Florence Tan's Best Nyonya Recipes

Kerabu Udang and Timun (Prawn and Cucumber Salad)

Serves 6

Medium-sized prawns (shrimps) 400 g (14 oz), boiled in salted water with shells until cooked

Spicy shrimp paste (*sambal belacan*) (page 112) 3 Tbsp

Sugar 4 Tbsp

Salt 1/2–3/4 tsp

Kasturi lime juice 3 Tbsp

Kaffir lime leaves 5, thinly sliced

Torch ginger bud (*bunga kantan*) 1 stalk, thinly sliced

Shallots 16, about 160 g (5 2/3 oz), peeled and thinly sliced

Cucumber 600 g (1 lb 5 2/5 oz), coarsely grated, core discarded (see picture below)

Garnishing

Peanuts 5 Tbsp, coarsely blended

Red chilli 1, thinly sliced

1. When prawns have cooled, shell and devein them.
2. Combine spicy shrimp paste, sugar, salt and lime juice.
3. Mix in kaffir lime leaves, torch ginger bud, shallots and prawns.
4. Add cucumber and mix.
5. Garnish with peanuts and sliced red chilli. Serve immediately.

NOTE

- In place of cucumber, vegetables such as bean sprouts, cabbage, ferns (*pucuk paku*) or banana blossoms (*jantung pisang*) can be used.
- If desired, add dried shrimps to spicy shrimp paste for extra texture.

Fried Squid à la Nyonya

This wonderful recipe was given by Dato' Chef Wan.

Serves 6–8

Cooking oil 4–5 Tbsp
Water 125 ml (4 fl oz / 1/2 cup)
Squid 750 g (1 lb 10 1/2 oz), cleaned, scored on the inside and cut into small pieces
Tomato sauce 2 Tbsp
Chilli sauce 2 Tbsp
Light soy sauce 1 Tbsp
Kasturi lime juice 1/2 Tbsp

Finely Ground Ingredients

Red chillies 5
Shallots 15, about 150 g (5 1/3 oz), peeled
Garlic 4 cloves, peeled
Ginger 1.25-cm (1/2-in) knob, peeled
Fresh turmeric 2.5-cm (1-in) knob, peeled
Lemon grass 2 stalks
Torch ginger bud (*bunga kantan*) 1 stalk
Shrimp paste (*belacan*) granules 1 tsp (See Note on page 20.)

Seasoning

Salt 3/4 tsp
Anchovy stock granules (*serbuk ikan bilis*) 1 tsp
Sugar 1 Tbsp

Garnishing

Mint leaves a handful

1. Heat oil in a wok. Fry finely ground ingredients until fragrant. Add water and simmer for 2 minutes.
2. Add squid, tomato sauce, chilli sauce and light soy sauce. Stir in seasoning. Cook for 3 minutes only.
3. Stir in lime juice.
4. Remove from heat and garnish with mint leaves. Serve immediately.

NOTE
- When washing the squid, retain some of the slime as it helps the squid curl nicely when cooked.

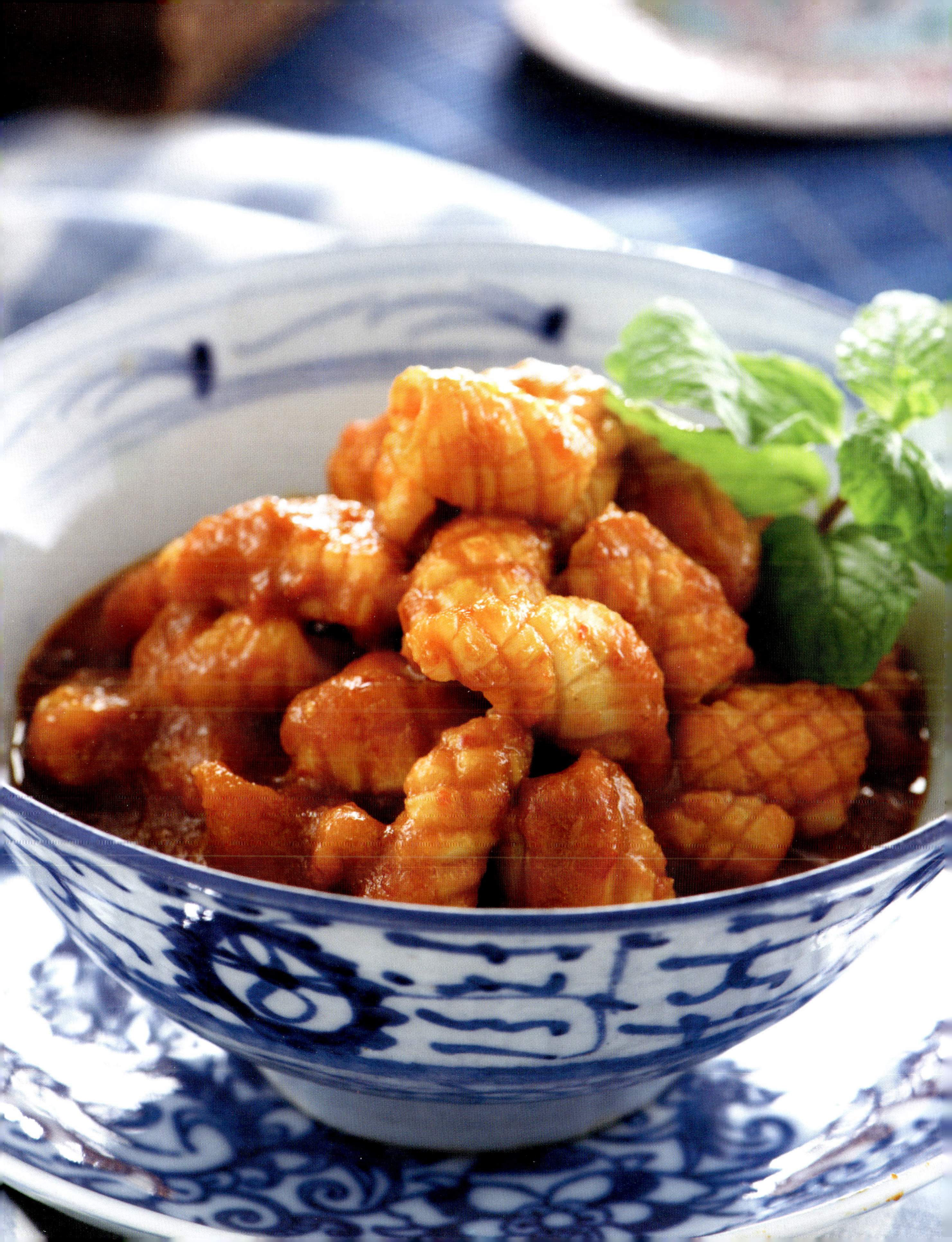

Nyonya Prawn (Shrimp) Porridge

Serves 6–8

Medium-sized prawns 500 g (1 lb 1½ oz), cleaned, shelled and deveined
Salt ⅛ tsp
Sugar ⅛ tsp
Ground white pepper ¼ tsp
Uncooked rice 200 g (7 oz), washed
Water 3 litres (101 fl oz / 12½ cups)
Firm beancurd (*tau kwa*) 4 pieces, cut into 2.5-cm (1-in) strips, fried until golden brown
Cooking oil 3 Tbsp
Chopped garlic 1 Tbsp

Seasoning

Dark soy sauce ¾ tsp
Light soy sauce 2½ Tbsp
Sugar 1 Tbsp
Salt 1 tsp
Anchovy stock 1 cube

Garnishing

Spring onions (scallions) 2 stalks, chopped
Shallot crisps (page 112) 2 Tbsp
Red chillies 2, sliced
Chopped preserved cabbage (*tung chye*) 2 Tbsp, washed

1. Marinate prawns with salt, sugar and pepper for 10 minutes.
2. Combine uncooked rice and water in a deep saucepan. Bring to a boil. Add fried beancurd and seasoning. Reduce heat to a simmer and cook porridge to a thick consistency.
3. Meanwhile, heat oil in a wok. Fry garlic until fragrant. Add marinated prawns and cook until the colour changes.
4. When porridge is thick, add prawns and cook for 1 minute.
5. Ladle porridge into serving bowls. Garnish with spring onions, shallot crisps, red chillies and chopped preserved cabbage. Serve hot.

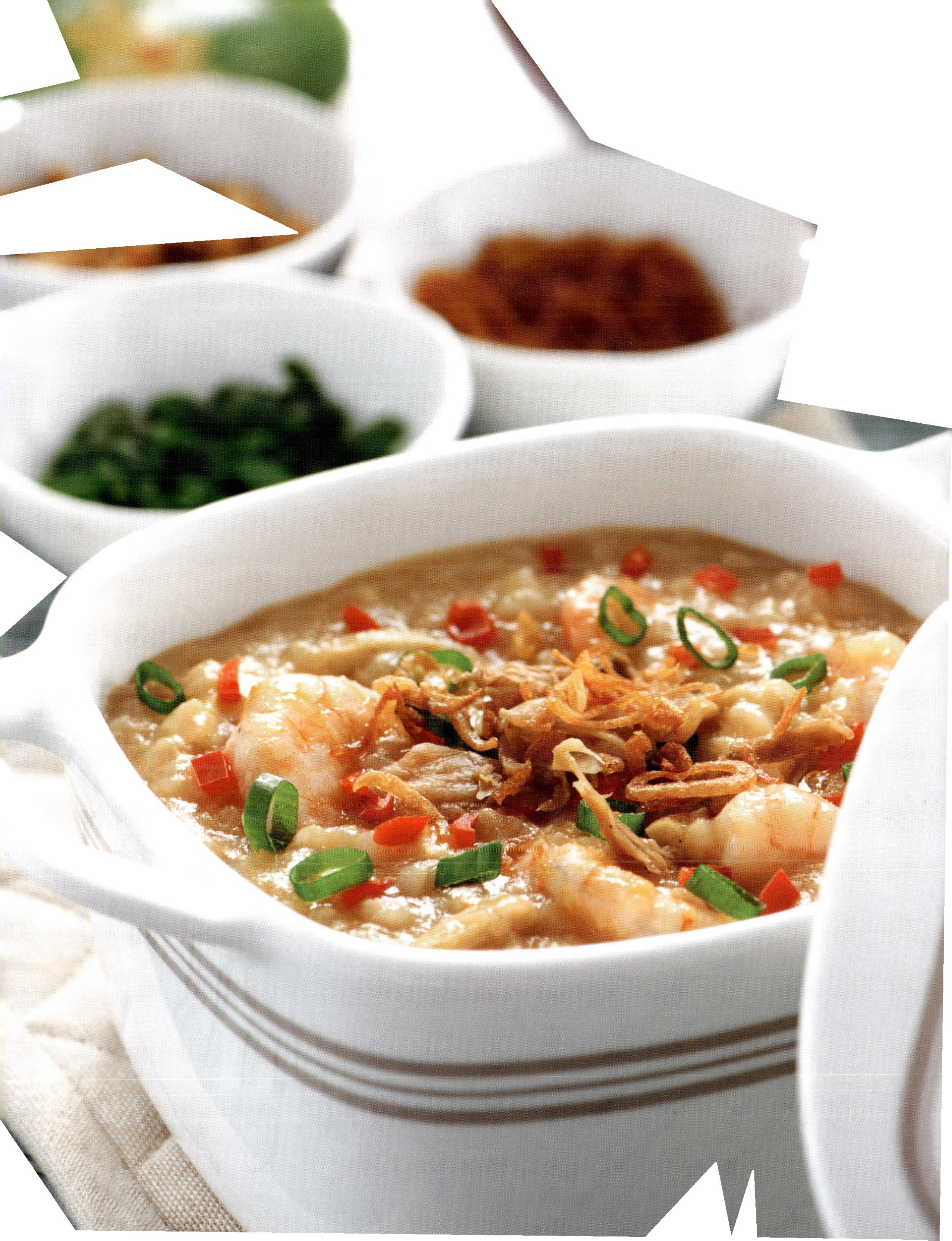

Spicy Prawn (Shrimp) Curry with Pineapple

Serves 8–10

Cooking oil 180 ml (6 fl oz / ¾ cup)
Fresh pineapple slices 500 g (1 lb 1½ oz), core removed and quartered
Sugar 1 Tbsp
Water 750 ml (24 fl oz / 3 cups)
Asam gelugur 1 slice
Kaffir lime leaves 5
Big prawns (shrimps) 1 kg (2 lb 3 oz), feelers removed and shells intact
Thick coconut milk (page 116) 350 ml (11¾ fl oz)

Finely Ground Ingredients

Dried red chillies 30, deseeded, soaked in boiling water in a covered bowl for 20 minutes until soft
Shallots 30, about 300 g (10½ oz), peeled
Garlic 4 cloves, peeled
Candlenuts (*buah keras*) 5
Galangal 2.5-cm (1-in) knob, peeled
Lemon grass 4 stalks
Shrimp paste (*belacan*) granules 2 tsp (See Note on page 20.)
Fresh turmeric 3.5-cm (1½-in) knob, peeled

Seasoning

Salt 1 Tbsp
Sugar 3 Tbsp
Fish stock granules 1 Tbsp

Garnishing

Lemon grass 1 stalk
Kaffir lime leaves 3

1. Heat oil in a wok. Fry finely ground ingredients until fragrant.
2. Add pineapples and cook for 3 minutes. Stir in 1 Tbsp sugar.
3. Add water and asam gelugur. Bring to a boil and add kaffir lime leaves. Lower heat and allow to simmer for 10 minutes.
4. Increase heat and add prawns, followed by the seasoning. When prawns are cooked, stir in coconut milk. Bring to a boil.
5. Garnish with lemon grass and kaffir lime leaves. Serve immediately with rice.

Seafood 61

Spicy Sweet and Sour Prawn (Shrimp) Curry

Serves 4–6

Cooking oil 125 ml (4 fl oz / 1/2 cup)

Curry leaves 3 sprigs

Curry paste 4 Tbsp curry powder mixed with 4 Tbsp water

Big onions 4, about 220 g (7 4/5 oz), peeled and sliced

Tamarind juice extracted from 50 g (1 2/3 oz) tamarind pulp and 400 ml (13 1/2 fl oz) water

Big prawns 700 g (1 1/2 lb), cleaned and deveined, feelers and shells removed

Red chilli 1, deseeded and cut into triangles (See Note on page 22.)

Green chilli 1, deseeded and cut into triangles

Finely Ground Ingredients

Dried red chillies 15, deseeded, soaked in boiling water in a covered bowl for 20 minutes until soft

Shallots 15, about 150 g (5 1/3 oz), peeled

Shrimp paste (*belacan*) granules 1 tsp (See Note on page 20.)

Seasoning

Salt 1 tsp

Light soy sauce 1 tsp

Sugar 3 Tbsp

1. Heat oil in a non-stick pan. Fry finely ground ingredients until fragrant. Add curry leaves and curry paste. Fry until fragrant.
2. Stir in big onions. Fry for 2 minutes. Add tamarind juice and bring to a boil.
3. Reduce heat and allow to simmer for 5 minutes. Add seasoning.
4. Increase heat and add prawns and chillies.
5. When prawns are cooked and curry is thick, remove from heat and serve immediately.

NOTE
- If desired, cook prawns with shells intact.

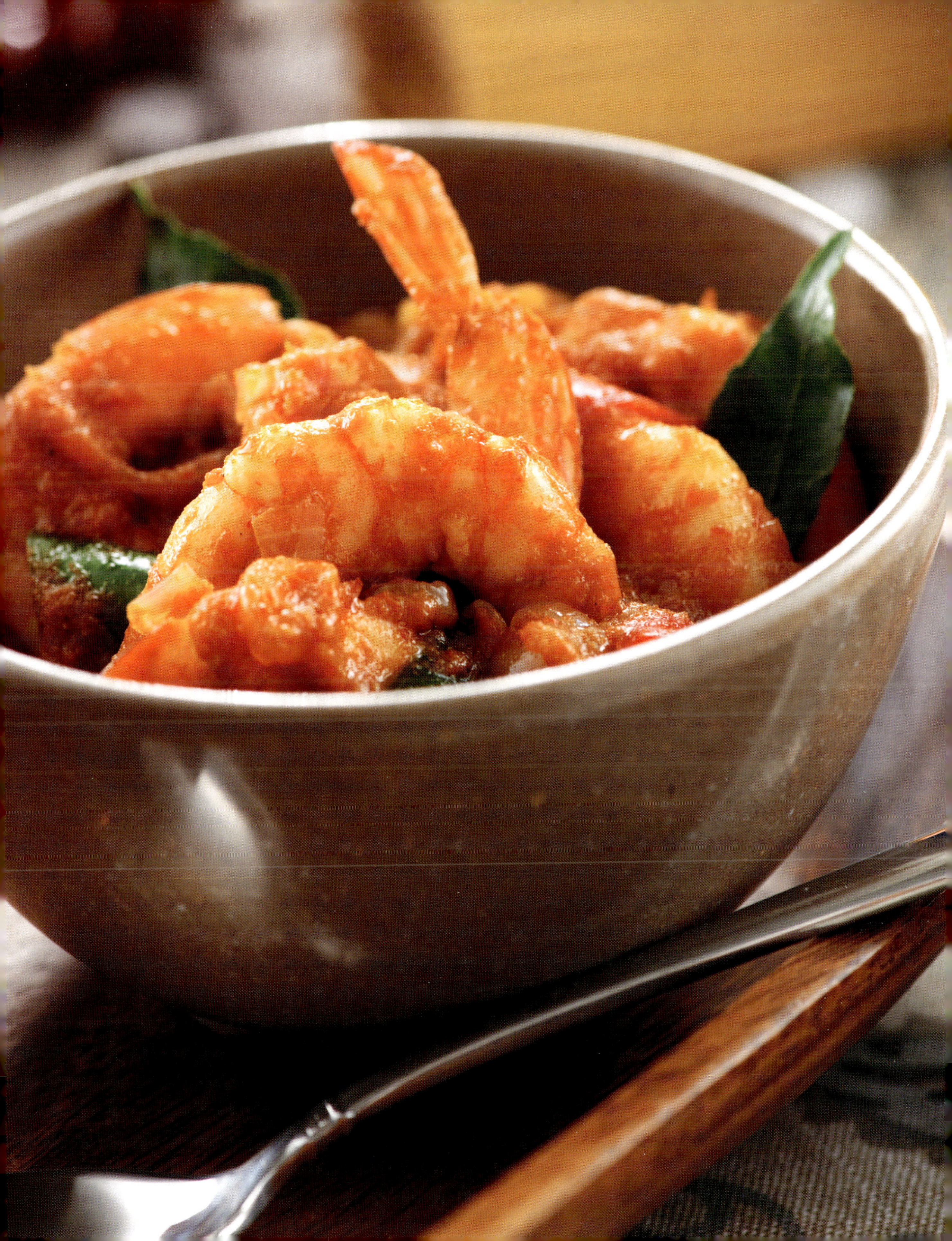

Sweet and Sour Squid

Serves 8–10

Dried shrimps 50 g (1 2/3 oz)

Cooking oil 4 Tbsp

Squid 1 kg (2 lb 3 oz), cleaned, scored on the inside and sliced at an angle (See Note on page 56.)

Finely Ground Ingredients

Young ginger 10 g (1/3 oz), peeled

Bird's eye chillies 10

Red chillies 3

Garlic 7 small cloves, peeled

Sauce

Chilli sauce 3 Tbsp

Tomato sauce 3 Tbsp

Vinegar 2 1/4 Tbsp

Sesame oil 1/2 tsp

Salt 1/4 tsp, heaped

Sugar 6 1/2 tsp

Garnishing

Mint leaves a handful

1. Rinse dried shrimps, then soak for 5 minutes. Process in a blender until finely blended. Set aside.
2. Heat oil in a wok. Sauté blended dried shrimps until fragrant. Transfer to a serving dish.
3. Prepare sauce. Mix finely ground ingredients with sauce and sautéed dried shrimps. Set spicy shrimp sauce aside.
4. Blanch squid with 3–4 Tbsp boiling water until cooked. Drain and immediately douse with cold water to give them a springy texture.
5. Drain well and mix with the spicy shrimp sauce prepared in step 3.
6. Garnish with mint leaves and serve immediately.

Seafood 65

Special Fried Prawns (Shrimps)

Serves 4

Big prawns (shrimps) 1 kg (2 lb 3 oz), cleaned, shelled and deveined with tails intact
Cornflour (cornstarch) 2 Tbsp
Cooking oil 600 ml (19 fl oz)

Seasoning
Salt 1/2 tsp
Sugar 2 tsp
Sesame oil 1 tsp
Ground white pepper 1/4 tsp
Egg white 1

Batter
Plain (all-purpose) flour 225 g (8 oz)
Wheat starch flour (*tang min fun*) 1 1/2 Tbsp
Custard powder 3/4 Tbsp
Baking powder 3/4 Tbsp
Salt 1/4 tsp, slightly heaped
Ground white pepper 1/4 tsp
Water 300 ml (10 fl oz / 1 1/4 cups)
Cooking oil 90 ml (3 fl oz / 3/8 cup)

Garnishing
Lettuce leaves a few

1. Pat dry prawns with a towel. Make three shallow cuts, each 0.5 cm (1/4 in) apart, along the underside of each prawn. The cuts should be parallel to the stripes on the prawn's body. Gently massage it straight.
2. Marinate prawns with seasoning for 10 minutes, then coat with cornflour.
3. Prepare batter. Sift flour, wheat starch flour, custard powder and baking powder together into a bowl. Mix in salt and pepper. Gradually pour in water and blend well with a whisk. Mix in oil and stir until well mixed.
4. Heat oil in a wok. Coat prawns in batter. Using chopsticks, hold each prawn by the tail, and lower it into the heated oil. Hold on to the prawn for awhile, until it stiffens slightly, before releasing it into the oil. Deep-fry until golden brown.
5. Remove from heat and drain off oil.
6. Garnish with lettuce leaves. Serve with chilli sauce.

NOTE
- Wheat starch flour can be bought from supermarkets or shops that sell pastry and baking products. If unavailable, cornflour may be used instead.

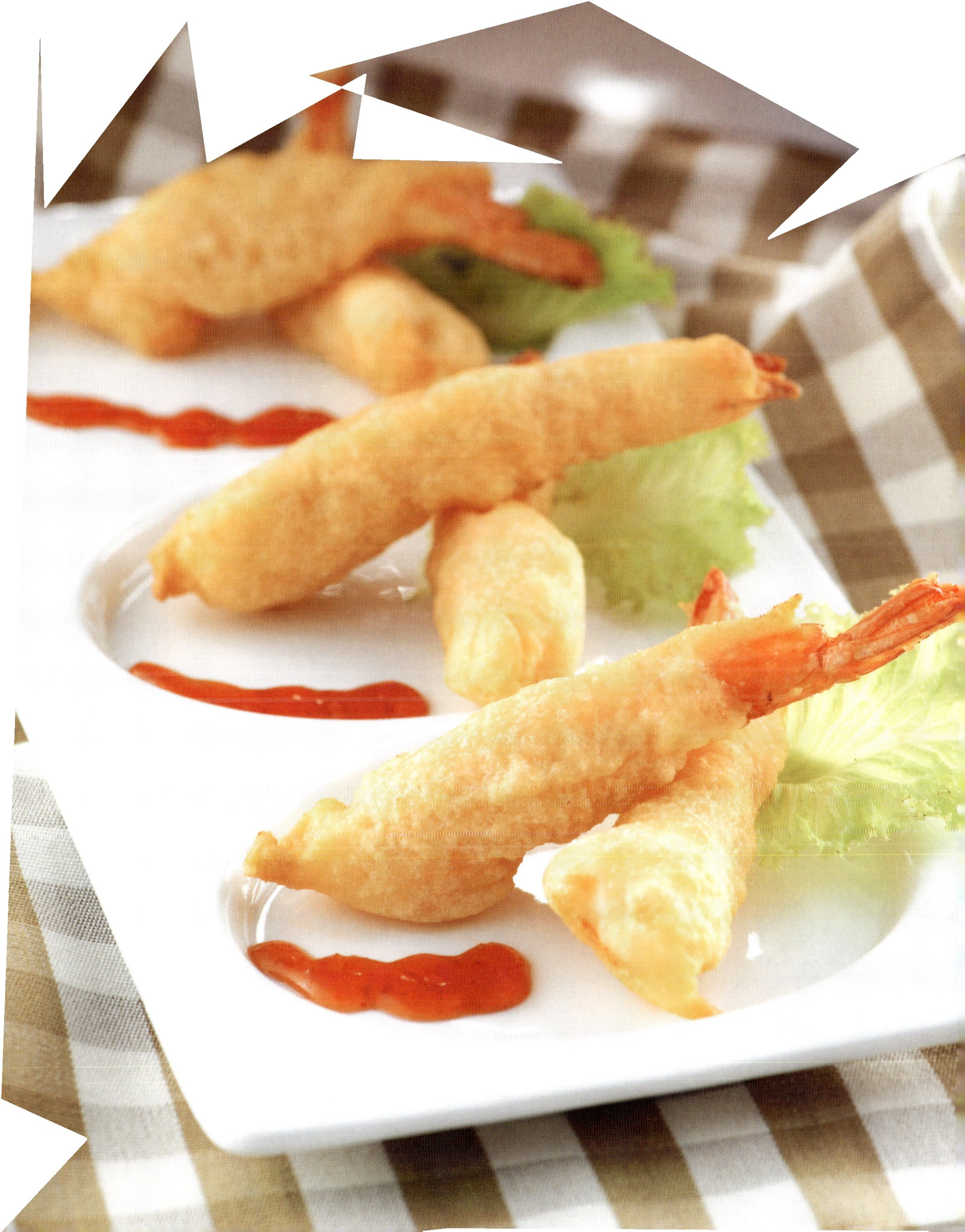

Sambal Prawns (Shrimps)

Serves 4–6

Cooking oil 100 ml (3 1/3 fl oz)
Medium-sized prawns 600 g (1 lb 5 2/5 oz), cleaned, shelled and deveined
Finely sliced kaffir lime leaves 1/2 Tbsp

Finely Ground Ingredients

Dried red chillies 15, deseeded, soaked in boiling water in a covered bowl for 20 minutes until soft
Red chillies 4
Shallots 12, about 120 g (4 1/3 oz), peeled
Shrimp paste (*belacan*) granules 1 tsp (See Note on page 20.)
Candlenuts (*buah keras*) 3

Seasoning

Salt 1 1/2 tsp
Sugar 2 1/2 Tbsp
Kasturi lime juice 40 ml (1 fl oz)

Garnishing

Kaffir lime leaves a handful + 1/2 Tbsp finely sliced

1. Heat oil in a non-stick pan. Fry finely ground ingredients until fragrant.
2. Add prawns and cook until they change colour. Stir in kaffir lime leaves and seasoning.
3. Garnish with kaffir lime leaves. Serve immediately with cucumber and rice if desired.

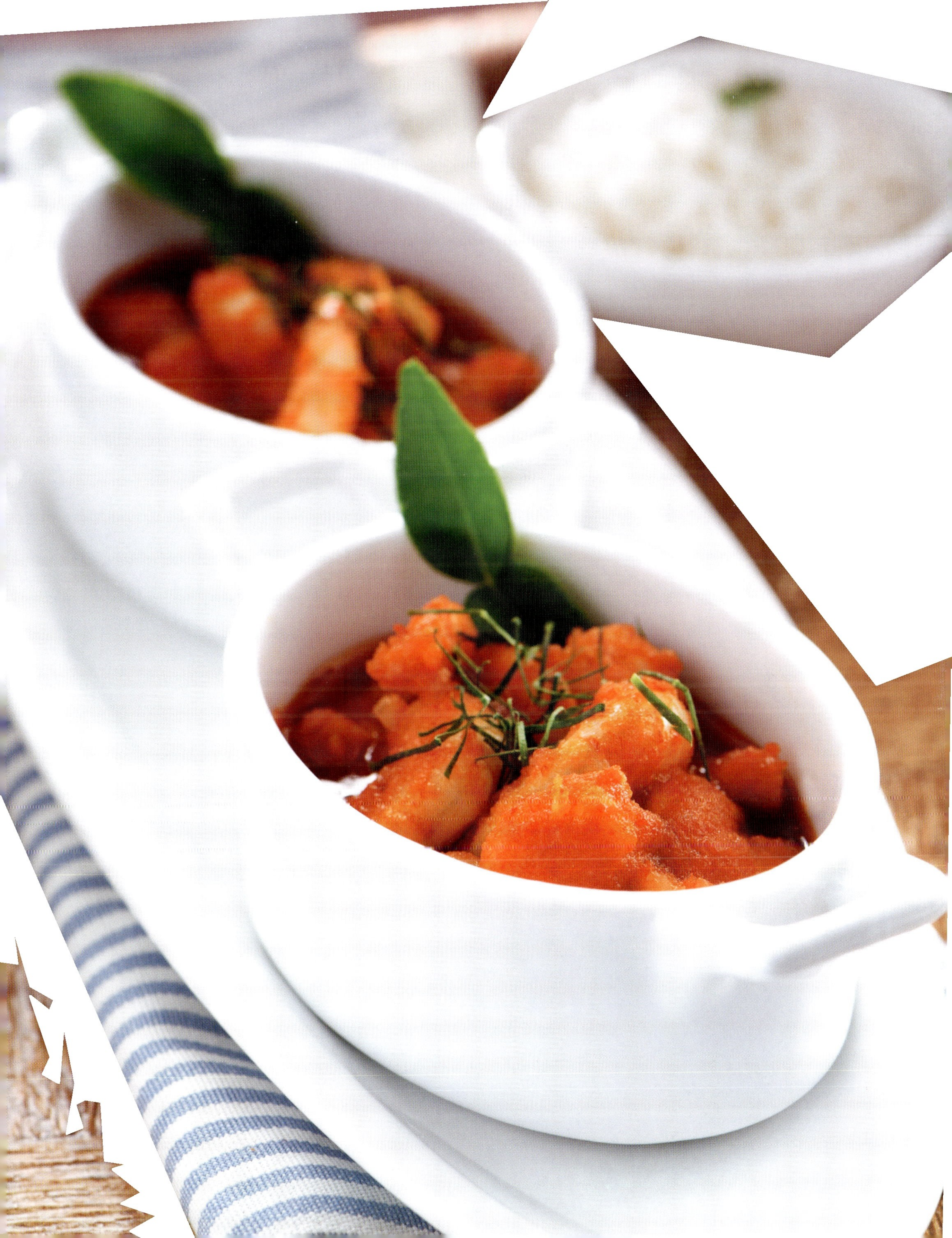

Eggplants with Spicy Shrimp Dip

Serves 4–5

Long eggplants (aubergines/brinjals) 2, about 600 g (1 lb 5$^{2}/_{5}$ oz)

Dip

Dark soy sauce 1 Tbsp

Kasturi lime juice 1$^{1}/_{2}$ Tbsp

Spicy shrimp paste (*sambal belacan*) (page 112) 3 Tbsp

Sugar 3$^{1}/_{2}$ tsp

Garnishing

Coriander (cilantro) leaves 1 sprig

1. Steam or grill eggplants until soft. Cut into 3-cm (1$^{1}/_{4}$-in) lengths and arrange on a serving plate.
2. Combine remaining ingredients to make spicy shrimp dip. Stir until well mixed.
3. Garnish eggplants with coriander leaves. Serve with dip.

Spicy Tofu Soup

Serves 4–5

Soft tofu 2 tubs, 300 g (10 1/2 oz) each
Cooking oil 2 1/2 Tbsp
Medium-sized prawns (shrimps) 200 g (7 oz), cleaned, shelled and deveined
Water 1.25 litres (40 fl oz / 5 cups)
Spring onions (scallions) 4 stalks, cut into 3-cm (1 1/4-in) lengths
Spicy shrimp paste (*sambal belacan*) (page 112) to taste

Finely Ground Ingredients
Red chilli 1
Shallots 4, about 40 g (1 1/3 oz), peeled
Shrimp paste (*belacan*) granules 1 tsp (See Note on page 20.)

Seasoning
Salt 1 tsp
Anchovy stock granules (*serbuk ikan bilis*) 1 tsp

1. Slice each tub of tofu into 8 pieces. Set aside.
2. Heat oil in a saucepan. Fry finely ground ingredients until fragrant.
3. Add prawns and fry until they change colour. Pour in water and bring to a boil.
4. Add seasoning and tofu. When boiling, add spring onions.
5. Remove from heat and serve with spicy shrimp paste.

Chap Chye

Serves 4

Fried bean curd puffs (*tau pok*) 80 g (2$^{4}/_{5}$ oz)

Cooking oil 3 Tbsp

Ginger 3-cm (1$^{1}/_{4}$-in) knob, peeled and thinly sliced

Store-bought red fermented bean curd (*nam yee*) 60 g (2 oz), mashed, 50 ml (1$^{2}/_{3}$ fl oz) sauce reserved

Lily buds (*kim chiam*) 30 g (1 oz), hard tips cut off, knotted and soaked for 30 minutes

Cloud ear fungus (*wan yee*) 25 g ($^{4}/_{5}$ oz), soaked in water until soft, rough patch at base cut away

Bean curd skin (*fu chok*) 55 g (2 oz), soaked in water until soft and cut into 7.5-cm (3-in) lengths

Water 450 ml (15 fl oz)

Carrots 110 g (4 oz), peeled and thinly sliced, or cut into decorative shapes if desired

Cabbage 500 g (1 lb 1$^{1}/_{2}$ oz), cut into small pieces

Transparent vermicelli (*tang hoon*) 35 g (1$^{1}/_{4}$ oz), soaked in water for 10 minutes and cut into 7.5-cm (3-in) lengths

Seasoning

Salt 1 tsp

Sugar 2 Tbsp

1. Blanch fried bean curd puffs in boiling water for 3 minutes. Drain and set aside to cool. Squeeze dry of water and cut into halves.
2. Heat oil in a wok. Fry ginger for 3 minutes. Add fermented bean curd and cook over low heat until fragrant. Add fermented bean curd sauce and cook for another 1 minute.
3. Add lily buds, cloud ear fungus and bean curd skin. Pour in water and bring to a boil over high heat.
4. Add carrots, cabbage and seasoning.
5. When bean curd skin is soft, add fried bean curd puffs and transparent vermicelli.
6. Remove from heat when cabbage is tender.
7. Serve immediately.

Vegetables 73

Pineapple Patchree

I love this wonderful recipe, which was handed to me by my consultant, mentor and idol, Dato' Lim Bian Yam.

Serves 4–6

Pineapple 1, about 650 g (1 lb 7 oz), husk and core removed
Cooking oil 125 ml (4 fl oz / ½ cup)
Star anise 2
Curry leaves 3 sprigs
Water 250 ml (8 fl oz / 1 cup)
Thick coconut milk (page 116) 200 ml (6¾ fl oz)

Finely Ground Ingredients

Dried red chillies 15, deseeded, soaked in boiling water in a covered bowl for 20 minutes until soft
Red chillies 3
Fresh turmeric 3-cm (1¼-in) knob, peeled
Coriander (cilantro) powder 4 Tbsp
Shallots 15, about 150 g (5⅓ oz), peeled

Seasoning

Sugar 2 Tbsp
Salt 1¾ tsp

Garnishing

Red chilli 1, deseeded and cut into triangles (See Note on page 22.)

1. Cut pineapple into quarters, then cut into 1.5-cm (¾-in) thick triangles.
2. Heat oil in a wok. Fry star anise, curry leaves and finely ground ingredients until fragrant.
3. Add pineapple slices and cook for about 5 minutes over low heat. Add seasoning and water. Bring to a boil.
4. Lower heat and simmer until pineapple slices are tender. Add coconut milk and stir constantly until it boils for 2 minutes. Remove from heat.
5. Garnish with red chilli and serve.

NOTE
- The pineapple should weigh about 650 g (1 lb 7 oz) after the husk and core have been removed.

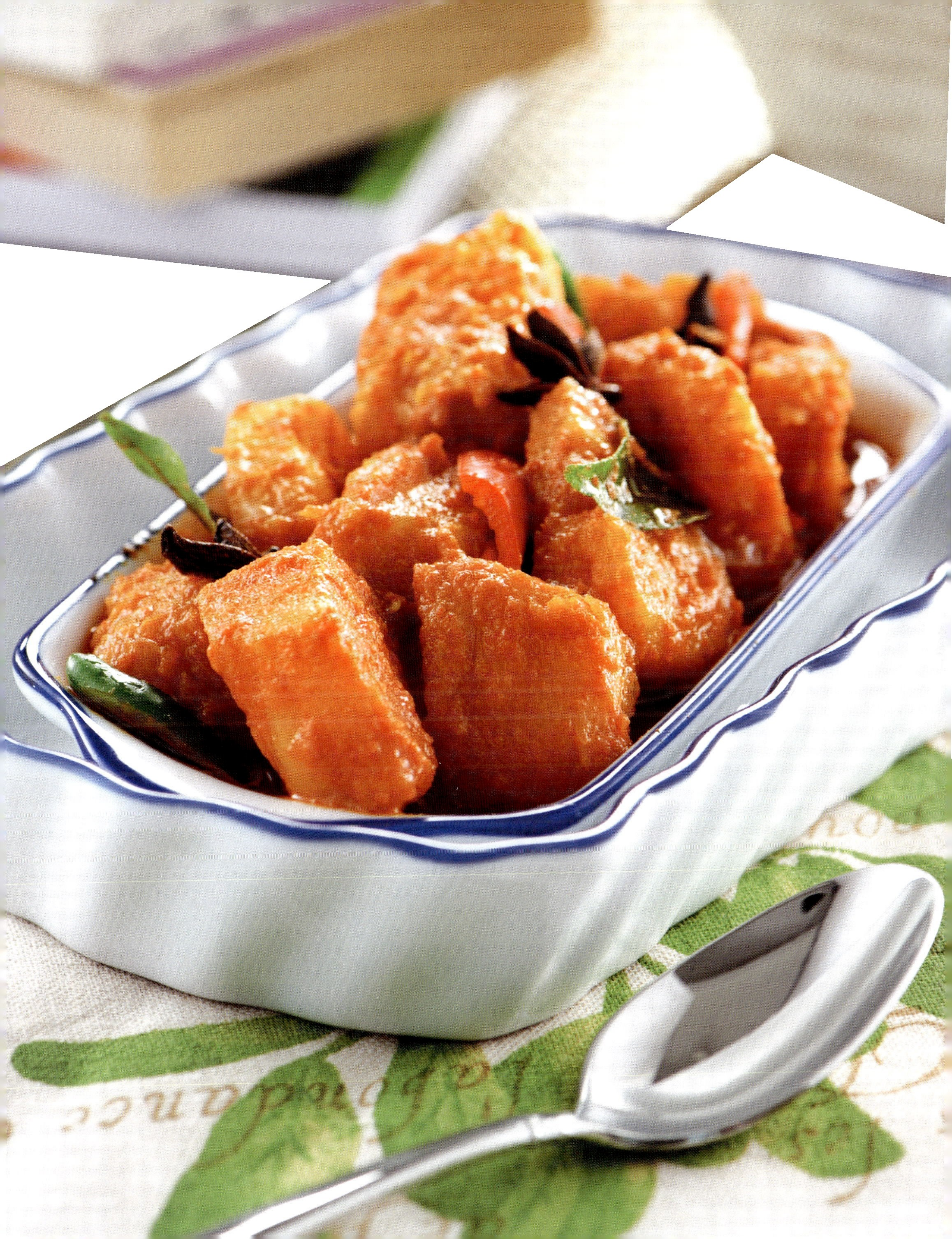

Kangkong Masak Lemak

Serves 2–4

Cooking oil 75 ml (2¹/₃ fl oz)
Prawns (shrimps) 200 g (7 oz), shelled, cleaned and deveined
Water 525 ml (16³/₄ fl oz)
Sweet potatoes 175 g (6¹/₄ oz), skinned and cut into 3.5-cm (1¹/₂-in) cubes
Water spinach (*kangkong*) 250 g (9 oz), cut into 4-cm (1³/₄-in) lengths
Thick coconut milk (page 116) 225 ml (7²/₃ fl oz)

Finely Ground Ingredients
Red chillies 5
Shallots 12, about 120 g (4¹/₃ oz), peeled
Shrimp paste (*belacan*) granules 1 tsp (See Note on page 20.)

Seasoning
Salt 1³/₄ tsp
Anchovy stock granules (*serbuk ikan bilis*) 1 tsp
Sugar 2 tsp

1. Heat oil in a wok. Fry finely ground ingredients until fragrant.
2. Add prawns and fry until they change colour. Pour in water and add sweet potatoes.
3. Cook until sweet potatoes are tender. Add water spinach and seasoning. Bring to a boil.
4. Stir in coconut milk. When water spinach is tender and coconut milk comes to a boil, remove from heat.
5. Serve immediately.

Vegetables 77

Kerabu Lady's Fingers

Serves 6

Young lady's fingers (okra) 400 g (14 oz)
Dried shrimps 60 g (2 oz), washed and soaked in boiling water for 5 minutes
Shallots 15, about 150 g (5$^1/_3$ oz), peeled and thinly sliced
Kaffir lime leaves 5, thinly sliced + more for garnishing
Torch ginger bud (*bunga kantan*) 1 stalk, thinly sliced + more for garnishing
Spicy shrimp paste (*sambal belacan*) (page 112) 4 Tbsp

Seasoning
Sugar 4 Tbsp
Kasturi lime juice 7$^1/_2$ tsp
Salt a pinch or to taste

1. Cook lady's fingers in boiling water for about 4 minutes. Drain and plunge into cold water to prevent further cooking. Remove the stems and ends. Slice diagonally into 4-cm (1$^3/_4$-in) lengths.
2. Process dried shrimps in a blender until finely blended. Combine blended dried shrimps with shallots, kaffir lime leaves, torch ginger bud, spicy shrimp paste and seasoning.
3. Mix in lady's fingers. Garnish with kaffir lime leaves and torch ginger bud. Serve immediately.

Vegetables 79

Mango Patchree

This is another wonderful recipe that I love from Dato' Lim Bian Yam.

Serves 4–6

Cooking oil 6 1/2 Tbsp

Curry leaves 3 sprigs

Sugar 2 Tbsp

Salt 3/4 tsp

Green chillies 3, deseeded and cut into triangles (see Note on page 22.)

Red chillies 3, deseeded and cut into triangles

Poached Mangoes (prepare a day in advance)

Small, unripe green mangoes 600 g (1 lb 5 2/5 oz), peeled and deseeded

Salted water 1 1/2 tsp salt dissolved in 1 litre (32 fl oz / 4 cups) water

Water 450 ml (15 fl oz)

Sugar 240 g (8 1/2 oz)

Salt 1 Tbsp

Finely Ground Ingredients

Dried red chillies 10, deseeded, soaked in boiling water in a covered bowl for 20 minutes until soft

Red chillies 3

Fresh turmeric 2.5-cm (1-in) knob, peeled

Coriander (cilantro) powder 4 Tbsp

Shallots 5, about 50 g (1 2/3 oz), peeled

1. Prepare poached mangoes a day in advance. Halve mangoes and soak in salted water for 15 minutes. Drain well and set aside.

2. Bring water, sugar and salt to a boil in a saucepan. When sugar has dissolved, add mangoes. Cover saucepan and remove from heat. Do not boil mangoes again or they will become too soft. Leave to cool overnight.

3. Heat oil in a wok. Fry finely ground ingredients and curry leaves until fragrant. Lower heat and add 5 Tbsp syrup from the poached mangoes, 2 Tbsp sugar and 3/4 tsp salt.

4. Add chillies and cook for 5 minutes. Remove from heat and add poached mangoes.

5. Leave curry to mature overnight before serving.

NOTE

- For best results, use unripe, sour mangoes for this recipe.
- The remaining mango syrup can be made into a drink by adding sugar to taste. It can be kept refrigerated for up to 1 week.

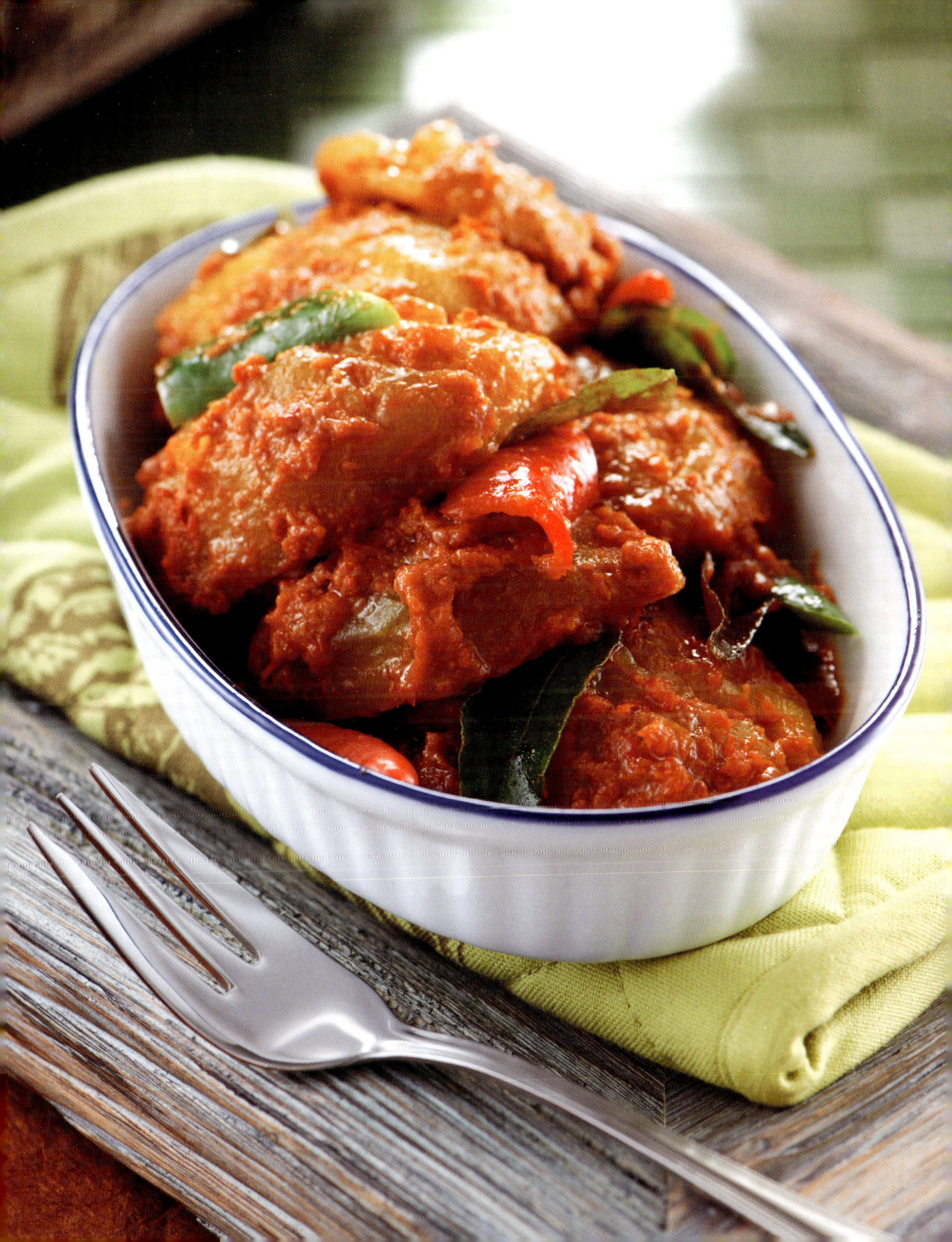

Mixed Vegetable Curry

Serves 4–6

Eggplant (aubergines/brinjals) 100 g (3 1/2 oz)
Fried bean curd puffs (*tau pok*) 8 pieces, about 100 g (3 1/2 oz)
Cooking oil 150 ml (5 fl oz)
Curry leaves 3 sprigs
Curry paste 7 Tbsp curry powder mixed with 7 Tbsp water
Water 1.5 litres (48 fl oz / 6 cups)
Potatoes 150 g (5 1/3 oz), peeled and quartered
Cabbage 200 g (7 oz), cut into small pieces
Carrots 120 g (4 1/3 oz), peeled and cut into 3-cm (1 1/4-in) lengths
French beans 150 g (5 1/3 oz), ends and string along the centre removed, cut into 3-cm (1 1/4-in) lengths
Red chilli 1, deseeded and cut into triangles (see Note on page 22.)
Green chilli 1, deseeded and cut into triangles
Medium-sized prawns (shrimps) 400 g (14 oz), cleaned, shelled and deveined
Thick coconut milk (page 116) 400 ml (13 1/2 fl oz)

Finely Ground Ingredients

Dried red chillies 8, soaked in boiling water in a covered bowl for 20 minutes until soft
Ginger 2-cm (3/4-in) knob, peeled
Fresh red chillies 2
Fresh turmeric 2.5-cm (1-in) knob, peeled
Shallots 18, about 180 g (6 1/3 oz), peeled
Ground white pepper 1/4 tsp
Shrimp paste (*belacan*) granules 1 tsp (See Note on page 20.)

Seasoning

Salt 2 1/4 tsp
Anchovy stock granules (*serbuk ikan bilis*) 1 1/2 tsp
Sugar 1/2 tsp

1. Cut eggplant into 3-cm (1¼-in) lengths. Halve each piece. Slit each half lengthwise, from one end to the centre. Soak in water until needed.
2. Blanch fried bean curd puffs in boiling water for 3 minutes. Drain and set aside to cool. Squeeze dry of water and cut into halves.
3. Heat oil in a wok. Fry curry leaves and finely ground ingredients until fragrant. Add curry paste and fry until fragrant. Pour in water.
4. Add potatoes and cook for 5 minutes. Add eggplant, cabbage, carrots and French beans. Bring to a boil.
5. Lower heat and simmer for 5 minutes. Add chillies, prawns, fried bean curd puffs and seasoning. Increase heat and cook for another 3 minutes.
6. Add coconut milk and bring to a boil.
7. Remove from heat and serve immediately.

Spicy Stuffed Bittergourd with Coconut Milk

Serves 4–6

Water 900 ml (30 fl oz) + 1.25 litres (40 fl oz / 5 cups) for cooking bittergourd
Bittergourd 300 g (10 1/2 oz), cut into 1.5-cm (3/4-in) rings, centre removed
Cooking oil 135 ml (4 2/3 fl oz)
Thick coconut milk (page 116) 250 ml (8 fl oz / 1 cup)
Spicy shrimp paste (*sambal belacan*) (page 112) to taste

Filling
Spanish mackerel flesh 250 g (9 oz), scraped from fish and blended to a paste
Salt 1/2 tsp
Iced water 2 1/2 Tbsp
Ground white pepper 1/8 tsp
Cornflour (cornstarch) 1/2 tsp

Finely Ground Ingredients
Shallots 15, about 150 g (5 1/3 oz), peeled
Garlic 2 cloves, peeled
Galangal 1.25-cm (1/2-in) knob, peeled
White peppercorns 15
Candlenuts (*buah keras*) 4
Lemon grass 2 stalks
Shrimp paste (*belacan*) **granules** 1 tsp (See Note on page 20.)
Fresh turmeric 3.5-cm (1 1/2-in) knob, peeled

Seasoning
Salt 1 1/4 tsp
Anchovy stock granules (*serbuk ikan bilis*) 3/4 tsp
Sugar 1 tsp

NOTE
• Ready-made fish paste can be bought from the wet market or supermarket.

1. Bring 1.25 litres (40 fl oz / 5 cups) water to a boil in a saucepan. Drop in bittergourd slices and cook for 10 minutes. Drain and set aside to cool.
2. Prepare filling. Place blended fish paste in a mixing bowl. In a separate bowl, combine the rest of the ingredients for the filling, then gradually add to the blended fish paste. Stir in one direction 15 times until the mixture becomes sticky.
3. Gather mixture and repeatedly hit it against a bowl 15 times until springy.
4. Lightly dab hands with oil. Gather about 1 Tbsp mixture and stuff into a bittergourd ring. Oil hands again and smoothen out filling. Place on a lightly greased plate to prevent sticking. Repeat until all bittergourd rings are used up.
5. Heat oil in a wok. Fry finely ground ingredients until fragrant. Pour in 900 ml (30 fl oz) water and bring to a boil. Lower heat and simmer for 5 minutes.
6. Add seasoning and stuffed bittergourd slices. Cook for 5 minutes.
7. Pour in coconut milk and stir slowly. When boiling, remove from heat.
8. Serve with spicy shrimp paste.

Cencaluk Omelette

Serves 4

Cencaluk 1 1/2 Tbsp, drained
Eggs 2
Spring onion (scallion) 1 stalk, sliced
Red chilli 1, deseeded and thinly sliced
Shallots 5, about 50 g (1 2/3 oz), peeled and thinly sliced
Cooking oil 1 1/2 Tbsp

Seasoning
Ground white pepper 1/8 tsp
Sesame oil 1/4 tsp

1. Lightly wash cencaluk to remove excess salt. Drain off water.
2. Lightly beat eggs with a fork. Add cencaluk, spring onion, red chilli, shallots and seasoning.
3. Heat oil in a non-stick pan. Pour in egg mixture and cook over low heat until golden brown. Turn over and cook the other side until golden brown.
4. Remove from heat and serve immediately.

NOTE
- Adjust amount of cencaluk according to taste. Use less if cencaluk is salty.

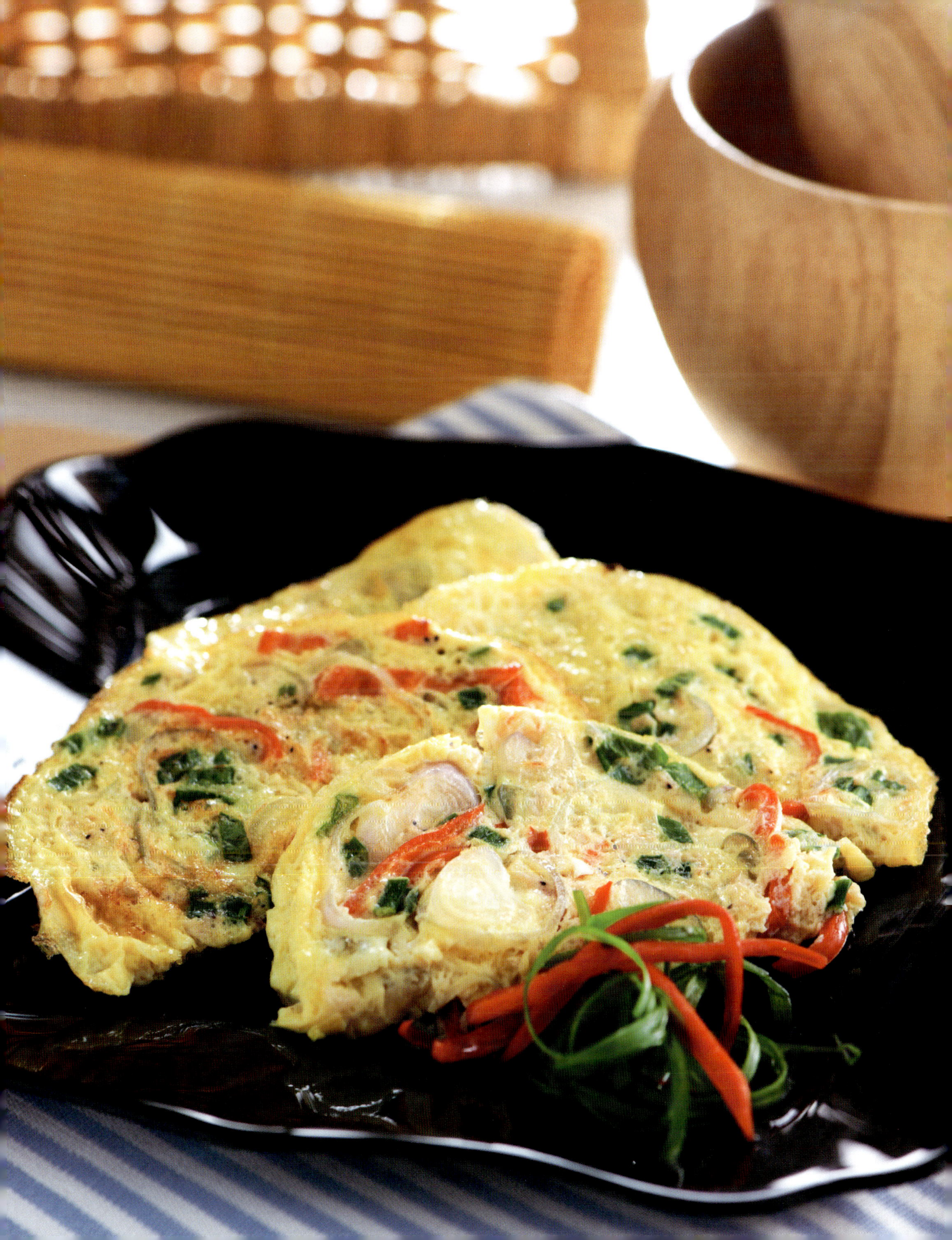

Bubur Caca

Serves 4–6

Sweet potatoes 325 g (11½ oz), ends removed, peeled and cut into 1-cm (½-in) cubes
Yam cubes 300 g (10½ oz), each 1 cm (½ in) in length
Water 700 ml (23½ fl oz)
Screwpine (pandan) leaves 4, knotted
Salt ¼ tsp
Thick coconut milk (page 116) 600 ml (19 fl oz)
Evaporated milk 100 ml (3⅓ fl oz)
Sugar to taste

Syrup
Dark brown palm sugar (*gula melaka*) 125-g (4½-oz) block, finely chopped
Screwpine (pandan) leaves 3, knotted
Water 150 ml (5 fl oz)

White Jelly
Tapioca flour 4 Tbsp, sifted
Boiling water 6½ tsp
Water 500 ml (16 fl oz / 2 cups), for cooking the white and blue jelly

Blue Jelly
Blue pea flower (*bunga telang*) juice (page 113) 1 tsp
Water 5½ tsp
Tapioca flour 4 Tbsp, sifted

Red Jelly
Red food colouring a few drops
Boiling water 6½ tsp
Tapioca flour 4 Tbsp, sifted
Water 500 ml (16 fl oz / 2 cups), for cooking the red jelly

1. Place sweet potatoes and yam onto a steaming tray. Steam until soft.
2. Prepare syrup. Heat palm sugar and screwpine leaves in water until sugar has dissolved. Pass through a sieve and discard screwpine leaves. Set aside.
3. Prepare white jelly dough. In a bowl, mix flour with boiling water. Stir vigorously with a wooden spoon until well combined and a sticky dough forms.
4. Dust hands with tapioca flour. On a well-floured flat plastic surface, roll dough into a long thin strip about 1 cm (½ in) thick. Using a spatula, cut dough into 1-cm (½-in) cubes. Dust cubes lightly with tapioca flour. Set aside.
5. Prepare blue jelly dough. Combine blue pea flower juice and water. Bring to a boil. Stir into flour immediately. Stir vigorously with a wooden spoon until well combined and a sticky dough forms.

NOTE
- I prefer to use the Kapal ABC brand for tapioca flour as it always guarantees good results.
- It is best to use a fresh amount of boiling water to cook each different-coloured dough cubes so that they don't stain one another.

88 *Florence Tan's Best Nyonya Recipes*

6. Repeat step 4.
7. Prepare red jelly dough. Combine a few drops of red food colouring with 6½ tsp boiling water. Stir into flour immediately. Stir vigorously with a wooden spoon until well combined and a sticky dough forms.
8. Repeat step 4.
9. Bring 500 ml (16 fl oz / 2 cups) water to a boil. Drop white dough cubes into boiling water. Cook until they float and become jelly. Remove jelly using a strainer. Douse jelly cubes with cold water. Leave jelly cubes in cold water until needed.
10. Repeat step 10 for the blue dough cubes, using the same water for cooking the white jelly.
11. Repeat step 10 for the red dough cubes, but use a fresh amount of 500 ml (16 fl oz / 2 cups) boiling water.
12. Combine 700 ml (23½ fl oz) water, syrup and screwpine leaves in a saucepan. Bring to a boil. Add steamed sweet potatoes and yam, salt, jelly cubes, coconut milk and evaporated milk. Add sugar to taste and bring to a boil.
13. Remove from heat. Serve warm or chilled.

Desserts 89

Kuih Cara with Coconut Sauce

Serves 6–8

Coconut juice 200 ml (6$^{3}/_{4}$ fl oz)
Sugar 100 g (3$^{1}/_{2}$ oz)
Screwpine (pandan) leaves 2, knotted
Instant yeast $^{1}/_{2}$ tsp
Sugar $^{1}/_{8}$ tsp
Warm water 2 Tbsp
Plain (all-purpose) flour 155 g (5$^{1}/_{3}$ oz)
Salt $^{1}/_{8}$ tsp
Egg 1, slightly beaten
Thick coconut milk (page 116) 160 ml (5$^{1}/_{3}$ fl oz)
Baking powder 1 tsp
Cooking oil 1 Tbsp

Coconut Sauce

Plain (all-purpose) flour 1$^{1}/_{2}$ tsp
Salt $^{1}/_{8}$ tsp
Thick coconut milk (page 116) 75 ml (2$^{1}/_{3}$ fl oz)
Water 75 ml (2$^{1}/_{3}$ fl oz)
Screwpine (pandan) leaf 1, knotted

1. Prepare syrup. Combine coconut juice, sugar and screwpine leaves in a saucepan. Bring to a boil. Remove from heat. Set aside until lukewarm.
2. Prepare yeast mixture. Dissolve yeast and sugar in warm water. Set aside for 10 minutes until frothy.
3. In the meantime, sift flour and salt together into a mixing bowl. Make a well in the centre. Pour beaten egg into the well. Add coconut milk gradually, stirring slowly at the same time. Mix until a smooth consistency is formed.
4. Mix in syrup. Stir until batter is smooth. Strain through a sieve. Add yeast mixture and stir until well mixed. Cover with a towel and leave in a warm place for 1 hour, until the batter doubles in size. Mix in baking powder.
5. Heat a brass apam mould and its cover separately over medium-low heat for 5 minutes. Lightly grease mould with oil. Leave the cover on the stove at all times to keep it heated.
6. Stir batter every time before pouring into a mould. Pour batter until mould is three-quarters full. Cook uncovered until bubbles appear. Cover mould for $^{1}/_{2}$–1 minute to cook the top of the apam. Kuih cara is cooked when it is firm and not sticky to the touch.
7. Serve with coconut sauce.

Coconut Sauce

1. Mix flour and salt in a bowl. Gradually stir in coconut milk and water until batter is smooth. Strain through a sieve.
2. Pour batter into a saucepan. Add screwpine leaf and cook over low heat, stirring until mixture boils.
3. Remove from heat and serve with kuih cara.

NOTE
- If traditional apam mould is not available, use a saucepan and its cover. Cook over low heat to prevent burning the bottom of the apam.

Kuih Genggang (Layered Cake)

Makes a 27-cm (11-in) cake

Sugar 375 g (13 oz)

Screwpine (pandan) leaves 5, knotted

Water 250 ml (8 fl oz / 1 cup)

Rice flour 360 g (12 3/4 oz)

Tapioca flour 60 g (2 oz)

Salt 1/2–3/4 tsp

Water 800 ml (27 fl oz)

Thick coconut milk (page 116) 500 ml (16 fl oz / 2 cups), extracted from 1.5 kg (3 lb 1 1/2 oz) grated coconut

Red food colouring a few drops + more for the last layer

Rose essence 1/4 tsp

Blue food colouring 3 Tbsp blue pea flower (*bunga telang*) juice (page 113) mixed with 1 Tbsp rice flour

1. Prepare syrup. Combine sugar and screwpine leaves with water. Heat until sugar dissolves. Remove screwpine leaves and set aside to cool.
2. Combine rice flour, tapioca flour and salt in a bowl. Slowly stir in syrup, water and coconut milk. Strain through a sieve and divide batter into three portions.
3. Add red food colouring and rose essence into one portion.
4. Add blue food colouring to the second portion of batter. Leave the last portion uncoloured.
5. Grease a 27-cm (11-in) steaming tray and pre-heat it for 5 minutes.
6. Stir uncoloured batter before pouring a third of it onto steaming tray. Cover with aluminium foil and steam over medium heat for 4 minutes or until cooked. Kuih will be opaque when done.
7. Remove foil and scratch surface with a fork. This is to help the different layers stick.
8. Repeat steps 6–7 for blue batter.
9. Repeat steps 6–7 for red batter.
10. Continue layering kuih to make nine layers altogether, ending with red batter. Add a few more drops of red food colouring to intensify the colour of the last layer.
11. Steam for another 35–45 minutes over low heat.
12. Leave to cool before cutting and serving.

NOTE
- I prefer to use the Teratai brand for rice flour as it always guarantees good results.
- If some drops of water fall onto the kuih, dab lightly with a cloth to remove the water, or the layers will not stick.
- Stir batter before pouring into steaming tray to ensure it is well-mixed.

Desserts 93

Kuih Keledek Goreng (Fried Sweet Potato Balls)

Serves 6

Sweet potato cubes 300 g (10½ oz)
Salt a pinch
Plain (all-purpose) flour 8 tsp
Cooking oil 600 ml (19 fl oz)

Filling

Cooking oil 2½ Tbsp
Garlic 3 cloves, peeled and minced
Shallots 3, about 50 g (1⅔ oz), peeled and minced
Fermented soy bean paste (*tau cheo*) 1 tsp
Chicken fillet 300 g (10½ oz), finely diced
Water 100 ml (3⅓ fl oz)
Coriander (cilantro) powder 1 Tbsp
Candied winter melon 100 g (3½ oz), finely diced
Toasted sesame seeds 2 tsp

Seasoning

Light soy sauce ½ tsp
Dark soy sauce 1 tsp
Ground white pepper ⅛ tsp
Salt ¼ tsp

1. Steam sweet potatoes until soft, then pound finely while they are still hot.
2. Prepare filling. Heat 2½ Tbsp oil in a saucepan. Fry garlic and shallots until fragrant. Add fermented soy bean paste and fry until fragrant over low heat.
3. Add chicken and cook for a few minutes. Stir in water, coriander powder and seasoning.
4. When chicken is tender and the gravy has dried, remove from heat. Mix in candied winter melon and sesame seeds. Set aside until needed.
5. Combine sweet potato paste, salt and flour. Knead until dough is soft and does not stick to your hands.
6. Roll a small portion of dough into a ball of about 3 cm (1¼ in) in diameter. Flatten it out and spoon 1½ Tbsp filling into the dough. Seal edges well and roll into a ball again. Repeat until all the dough has been used up.
7. Heat oil to deep-fry sweet potato balls until golden brown.
8. Serve immediately.

NOTE
- Do not mash or blend sweet potatoes in a blender, or the texture will be affected.
- Use a small sieve to remove floating residue during frying.
- Leftover filling can be kept frozen for 1–2 weeks.

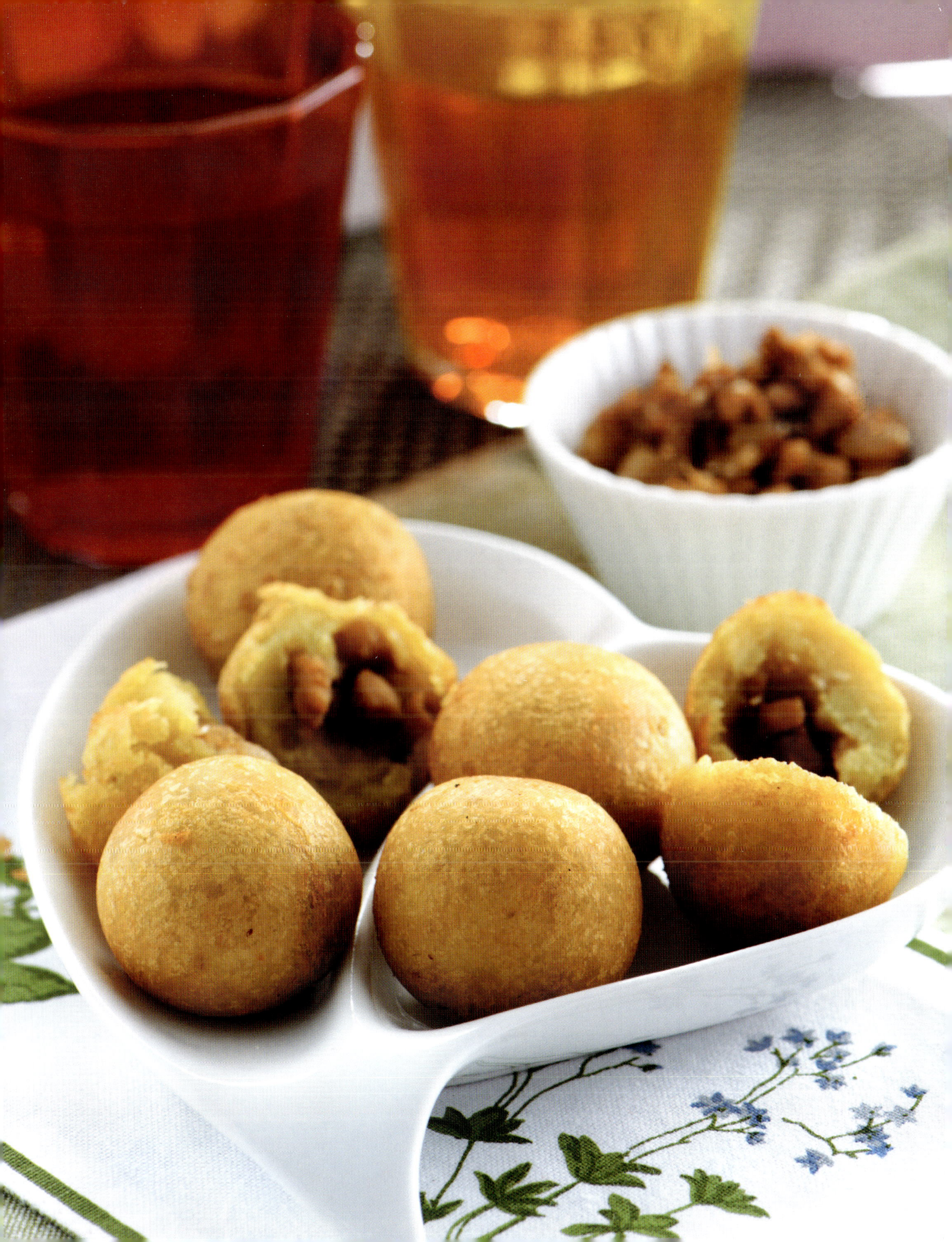

Kuih Kosui

Makes a 27-cm (11-in) cake

Palm sugar (*gula melaka*) 450 g (1 lb), finely chopped
Sugar 2 Tbsp
Coconut juice 200 ml (6$^{3}/_{4}$ fl oz)
Screwpine (pandan) leaves 5, knotted
Rice flour 180 g (6$^{1}/_{3}$ oz)
Tapioca flour 120 g (4$^{1}/_{3}$ oz)
Plain (all-purpose) flour 4 Tbsp
Water 1.15 litres (39 fl oz)
Alkaline water 3$^{1}/_{2}$ tsp
Grated coconut 200 g (7 oz), mixed with $^{1}/_{4}$ tsp salt

1. Prepare syrup. Combine palm sugar, sugar, coconut juice and screwpine leaves in a saucepan. Heat until sugars have dissolved. Strain through a sieve and set aside to cool.
2. Grease a 27-cm (11-in) steaming tray and pre-heat it for 5 minutes.
3. Meanwhile, mix rice flour, tapioca flour and plain flour in a bowl. Slowly pour in syrup, followed by water and alkaline water. Stir until well combined. Strain through a sieve, then stir over low heat until hot.
4. Pour mixture into heated steaming tray and cover with heavy duty aluminium foil. Close lid over steamer and steam for 35–40 minutes over low heat.
5. Remove from heat and set aside to cool.
6. Cut into slices and coat with grated coconut before serving.

Bubur Pulut Hitam (Black Glutinous Rice Porridge with Dried Longans)

Serves 8–10

Black glutinous rice 300 g (10 1/2 oz), washed and soaked overnight

Water 3.5 litres (118 fl oz / 14 3/4 cups)

Rock sugar 150 g (5 1/3 oz)

Palm sugar (*gula melaka*) 70 g (2 1/2 oz)

Dried longans 100 g (3 1/2 oz), washed

Thick coconut milk (page 116) 500 ml (16 fl oz / 2 cups), mixed with 1 tsp salt

1. Cook black glutinous rice in water until soft.
2. Add rock sugar, palm sugar and dried longans. Cook for 25 minutes. Longans are slightly firm, but will soften after about 1 hour.
3. Ladle into serving bowls and serve with coconut sauce.

Coconut Sauce

1. Cook coconut milk over medium-low heat, stirring continuously until it boils.
2. Remove from heat and serve with bubur pulut hitam.

Kuih Talam

Makes a 26-cm (10-in) cake

Bottom Layer

Screwpine (pandan) leaves 15, shredded
Water 500 ml (16 fl oz / 2 cups)
Rice flour 180 g (6$^{1}/_{3}$ oz)
Green pea flour 30 g (1 oz)
Water 340 ml (11$^{1}/_{2}$ fl oz)
Salt $^{1}/_{8}$ tsp
Alkaline water 1$^{1}/_{4}$ tsp
Sugar 250 g (9 oz)

Top Layer

Rice flour 75 g (2$^{2}/_{3}$ oz)
Cornflour (cornstarch) 30 g (1 oz)
Salt 1 tsp
Sugar $^{1}/_{4}$ tsp
Water 350 ml (11$^{3}/_{4}$ fl oz)
Thick coconut milk (page 116) 350 ml (11$^{3}/_{4}$ fl oz)

1. Prepare bottom layer of kuih. Process screwpine leaves and water in a blender. Strain through a sieve.
2. Grease a 26-cm (10-in) steaming tray and pre-heat it for 5 minutes.
3. Mix flours, water and salt. Combine with screwpine leaves mixture. Stir in alkaline water and sugar. Strain mixture through a sieve into a saucepan. Using a whisk, stir constantly over low heat until hot.
4. Quickly pour into heated tray. Cover with heavy duty aluminium foil. Dry steamer lid and close over steamer. Steam over low heat for 40–45 minutes or until cooked. Kuih will be opaque when done.
5. Meanwhile, mix all ingredients for top layer. Strain through a sieve. Using a whisk, stir constantly over low heat until hot.
6. When bottom layer is cooked, remove foil and scratch surface with a fork. This is to help the different layers stick.
7. Slowly pour in batter for top layer over the cooked bottom layer. Cover with heavy duty aluminium foil. Dry steamer lid and close over steamer. Steam over low heat for 40–45 minutes or until cooked. Kuih will be opaque when done.
8. Remove from heat. Allow to cool before cutting and serving.

NOTE
- Kuih Talam should be steamed over low heat to ensure a smooth surface.
- If water droplets appear on the kuih after steaming, use a kitchen paper towel to lightly dab away the water.

Desserts 99

Pang Susi

Makes 20 buns

Bread
Plain (all-purpose) flour 600 g (1 lb 5$^{2}/_{5}$ oz), sifted

Steamed sweet potato cubes (light yellow variety) 300 g (10$^{1}/_{2}$ oz), finely pounded

Salt $^{1}/_{4}$ tsp

Castor sugar 150 g (5$^{1}/_{3}$ oz)

Instant yeast 4 tsp

Egg yolks 2

Water 8 Tbsp, warm if using hands to knead

Melted butter 130 g (4$^{2}/_{3}$ oz)

Eggwash 1 egg, beaten

Filling
Cooking oil 3$^{1}/_{2}$ Tbsp

Big onions 2, about 150 g (5$^{1}/_{3}$ oz), finely diced

Chicken fillet 400 g (14 oz), finely diced

Potatoes 600 g (1 lb 5$^{2}/_{5}$ oz), peeled and finely diced

Water 300 ml (10 fl oz / 1$^{1}/_{4}$ cup) + more if potatoes are of a firmer variety

Ground white pepper $^{1}/_{4}$ tsp

Five-spice powder 2$^{1}/_{2}$ tsp

Seasoning
Chicken stock granules 1$^{1}/_{4}$ tsp

Salt 1 tsp

Sugar 4$^{3}/_{4}$ Tbsp

Light soy sauce 1 Tbsp

1. Prepare filling. Heat oil in a saucepan. Fry big onions for 3 minutes. Add chicken and cook for another 3 minutes. Add potatoes and fry for 1–2 minutes.

2. Add water, pepper, five-spice powder and seasoning. Cook until chicken and potatoes are tender, and gravy has dried. It should be similar to curry puff filling. Remove from heat and set aside to cool.

3. Prepare bread dough. Combine all ingredients for bread, except butter and eggwash, in a mixer; do not add salt, sugar and instant yeast in close succession. Using a dough hook, knead for 1 minute. Add butter and continue kneading at a higher speed for 15 minutes. Add a few drops of water if dough is too hard. Dough is ready when it stretches like a balloon. If not, continue kneading for another 5 minutes. Test stretchiness of dough again to make sure it is ready.

4. Remove from mixer and form into a ball. Place dough into a greased bowl. Cover with a cloth. Set under the sun or in a warm place to prove until the dough doubles in size. To test if dough is ready, press a finger into the dough. There should be a dent. Otherwise, continue to prove until dough is ready.

5. Punch dough down and knead for about 2 minutes. Divide dough into 20 pieces, each about 30 g (1 oz). Shape into balls and flatten each one with a rolling pin.

6. Spoon about 1½ Tbsp filling onto one half of flattened dough. Bring the other half over filling and crimp edges such that it looks like a curry puff. Turn over and shape pastry into an oval. Place on a lightly-floured tray and cover with a cloth. Leave aside for 30 minutes to let it rise. Repeat until all dough pieces have been used up.

7. Preheat oven to 180°C (350°F).

8. Glaze pastry with eggwash and bake for 25–30 minutes or until golden brown.

9. Remove from oven and leave to cool on a rack before serving.

NOTE
- Leftover filling can be kept frozen for 1–1½ weeks.

Talam Keladi

Makes a 25-cm (10-in) cake

Bottom Layer

Salt 1 tsp

Yam cubes 650 g (1 lb 7 oz), each 1 cm (1/2 in) in length

Screwpine (pandan) leaves 5, knotted

Banana leaf 1, for pressing yam

Top Layer

Sugar 120 g (4 1/3 oz)

Eggs 4

Plain (all-purpose) flour 3 Tbsp

Salt a pinch

Thick coconut milk (page 116) 275 ml (9 1/3 fl oz)

Water 100 ml (3 1/3 fl oz)

Yellow food colouring a few drops

Screwpine (pandan) leaves 3, knotted

1. Prepare bottom layer of kuih. Sprinkle salt over yam. Steam yam with screwpine leaves over high heat until yam becomes tender.
2. Grease a 25-cm (10-in) steaming tray.
3. Move yam to heated tray and press with a banana leaf until yam is firmly packed. Steam for another 8 minutes.
4. Prepare top layer of kuih. Lightly stir sugar into eggs. Combine flour and salt in another bowl. Slowly pour egg mixture into flour mixture.
5. Mix in coconut milk, water and food colouring. Stir until well combined. Strain through a sieve into a saucepan. Add screwpine leaves and stir constantly over low heat until mixture is hot.
6. Remove screwpine leaves. Slowly pour mixture over bottom layer of yam. Cover with heavy duty aluminium foil. Dry steamer lid and close over steamer. Steam over low heat for 40–45 minutes or until cooked. Kuih will be opaque when done.
7. Remove from heat and allow to cool before cutting and serving.

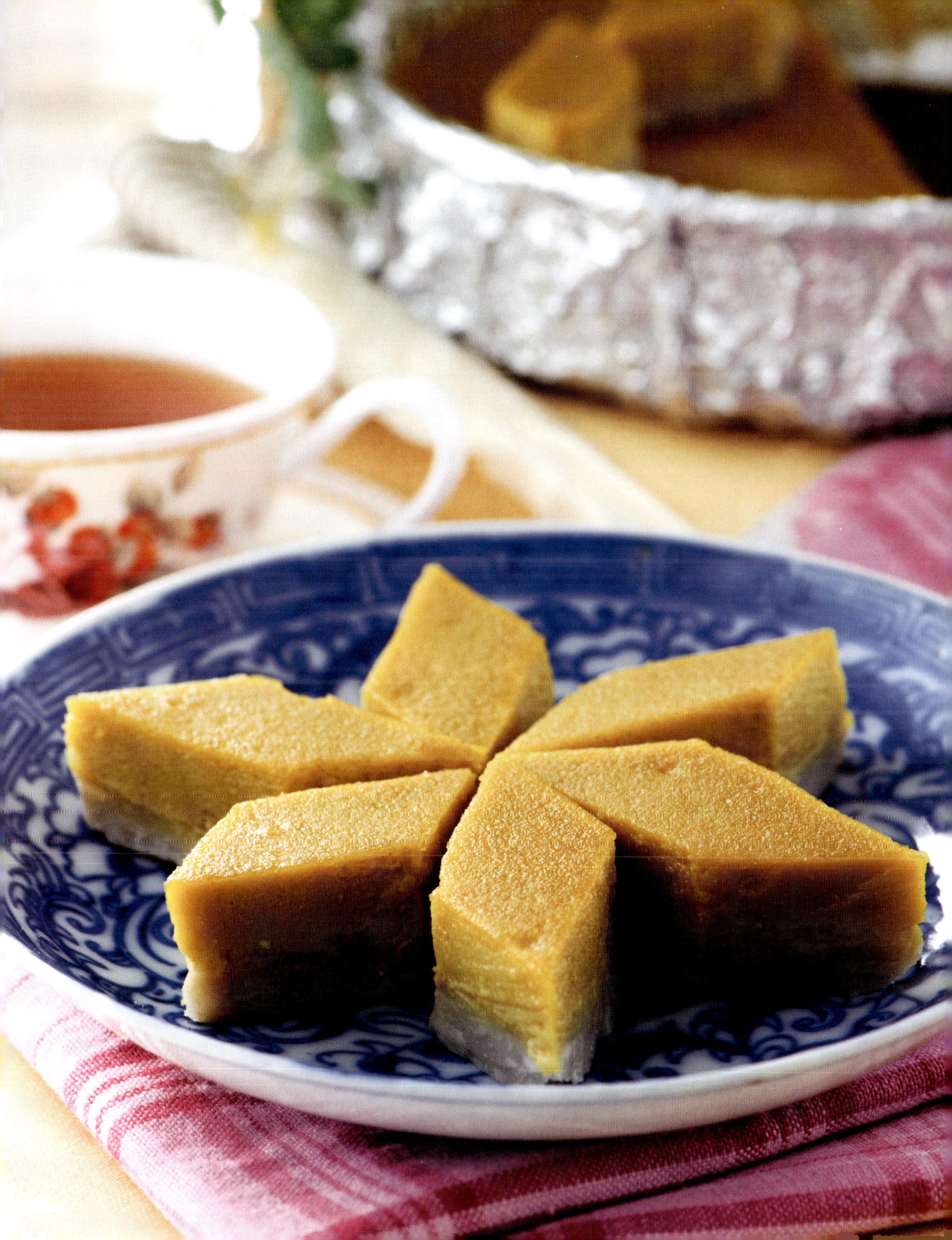

Kuih Bongkong

Makes 14 parcels

Rice flour 100 g (3 1/2 oz)
Salt 1 1/8 tsp
Thick coconut milk (page 116) 550 ml (18 2/3 fl oz)
Water 850 ml (29 fl oz)
Screwpine (pandan) leaves 5, knotted
Palm sugar (*gula melaka*) 100 g (3 1/2 oz), finely chopped
Sugar 2 Tbsp
Banana leaves 14, each 20 x 23 cm (8 x 9 1/4 in), washed, scalded and wiped dry
Screwpine (pandan) leaves 14, each 3 x 3 cm (1 1/4 x 1 1/4 in)
Banana leaves 14, each 4 x 15 cm (1 1/2 x 6 in), washed, scalded and wiped dry
Strong toothpicks 14

1. Mix rice flour and salt in a bowl. Gradually add in coconut milk, followed by water.
2. Strain through a sieve into a saucepan. Add screwpine leaves and cook over low heat, stirring constantly until batter boils and thickens. Remove from heat and discard screwpine leaves.
3. Mix palm sugar and sugar in a bowl.
4. Place a 20 x 23 cm (8 x 9 1/4 in) banana leaf on a plate. Scoop 2 Tbsp batter onto the centre of banana leave. Scoop 1 Tbsp sugar mixture over batter. Top with another 1 1/2 Tbsp batter. Place a screwpine leaf on top.
5. Fold leaves over batter as shown in the pictures below. Use a 4 x 15 cm (1 1/2 x 6 in) banana leaf to wrap around the folded bundle before fastening with a toothpick. Using scissors, trim off excess banana leaf.
6. Repeat steps 4–5 until all ingredients are used up.
7. Steam kuih bongkong over high heat for 20–25 minutes.
8. Serve warm or chilled.

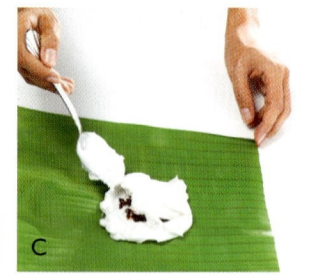

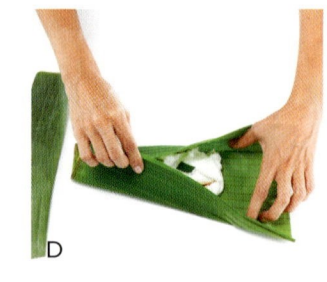

A B C D
E F G H

104 *Florence Tan's Best Nyonya Recipes*

Desserts 105

Buah Melaka

Serves 6

Screwpine (pandan) leaves 10, shredded
Water 100–170 ml (3$^{1}/_{3}$–5$^{3}/_{4}$ fl oz)
Glutinous rice flour 150 g (5$^{1}/_{3}$ oz)
Boiled sweet potatoes (light yellow variety) 100 g (3$^{1}/_{2}$ oz), pounded finely when hot
Green colouring (optional) a few drops

Filling
Palm sugar (*gula melaka*) 70 g (2$^{1}/_{2}$ oz), finely chopped
Castor sugar 1 Tbsp

Coating
Grated young coconut 100 g (3$^{1}/_{2}$ oz)
Salt $^{1}/_{4}$ tsp

1. Process screwpine leaves and water in a blender. Strain through a sieve and reserve juice.
2. Prepare filling. Mix palm sugar and castor sugar in a bowl.
3. Combine glutinous rice flour and sweet potatoes in a bowl. Gradually pour in screwpine juice and mix at the same time, until dough is soft and pliable. Do not add anymore screwpine juice if dough is of desired consistency. The dough should not stick to your hands. Add green food colouring if desired.
4. Scoop 1 tsp of dough and roll into a ball. Flatten it. Scoop about $^{1}/_{2}$ tsp filling onto the centre of dough and seal it. Repeat until all the dough and filling are used up.
5. Drop into half a saucepan of boiling water. When dough floats, cook for another 1 minute.
6. Meanwhile, prepare coating. Combine grated coconut with salt in a bowl. Steam for 5 minutes.
7. When buah melaka is ready, drain liquid and drop into coating. Coat buah melaka evenly and serve.

NOTE
• Be careful not to overcook the sweet potatoes or they will turn mushy.

Desserts 107

Apam Manis

Makes about 16 apam

(A)
Cold cooked rice 200 g (7 oz)
Finely ground and sifted round ragi yeast 3/4 tsp
Sugar 1 1/2 tsp

(B)
Sugar 200 g (7 oz)
Rice flour 240 g (8 1/2 oz)
Water 390 ml (13 fl oz)

(C)
Eno fruit salt 1/2 tsp
Double action baking powder 1/2 tsp
Food colouring of desired colour (optional) a few drops

1. Mix all ingredients in (A) in a clean container. Close lid over container and wrap with a towel. Set aside to ferment for 24 hours.
2. Scoop 180 g (6 1/3 oz) fermented rice into a blender. Add all ingredients in (B). Process until mixture is very smooth. Place into a container, cover and leave to ferment for 6–8 hours.
3. Line a mould of 6.5 cm (2 1/2 in) in diameter with paper cups. Space them evenly on the steaming tray.
4. Heat a steamer filled with three-quarters water. Bring water to a boil.
5. Meanwhile, mix ingredients in (C) into the fermented mixture in step 2. Stir quickly and vigorously until the raising agents, especially Eno fruit salt, have dissolved.
6. Quickly pour batter into moulds until they are full. Steam over high heat for 15–20 minutes or until cooked. Kuih will be opaque when done.
7. Remove from moulds and leave to cool before serving.

NOTE
- Place round ragi yeast in the sun for 2–3 days to ensure it is dry.
- Eno fruit salt must be completely dissolved, or yellow specks will appear on the cooked apam.
- Lining the apam mould with paper cups makes it easier to remove the apam later. It is important to space the apam evenly so that the heat is evenly distributed, allowing the batter to rise properly and form its distinctive flower-shaped appearance when cooked.
- Steam all apam at once instead of in batches for best results.

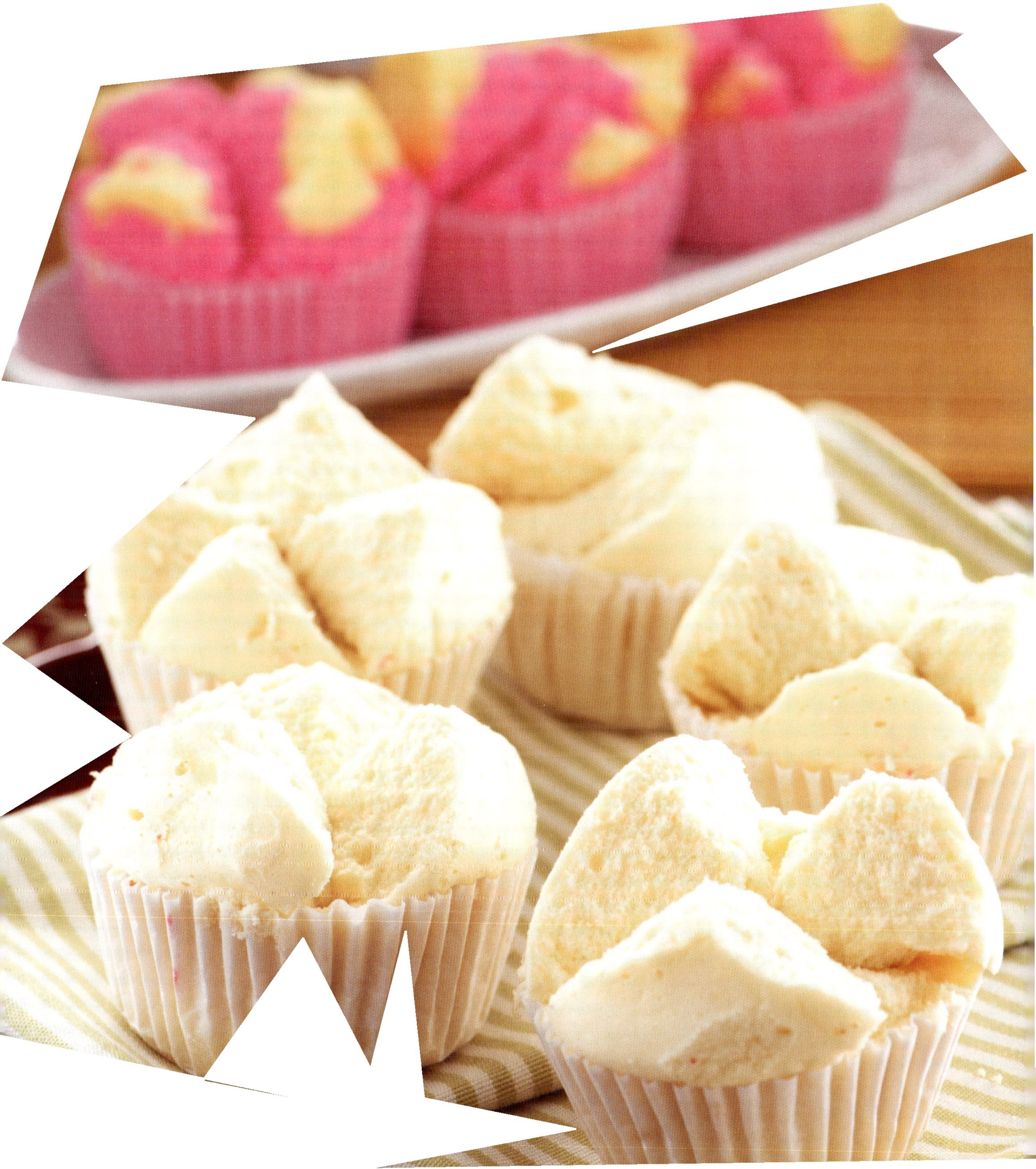

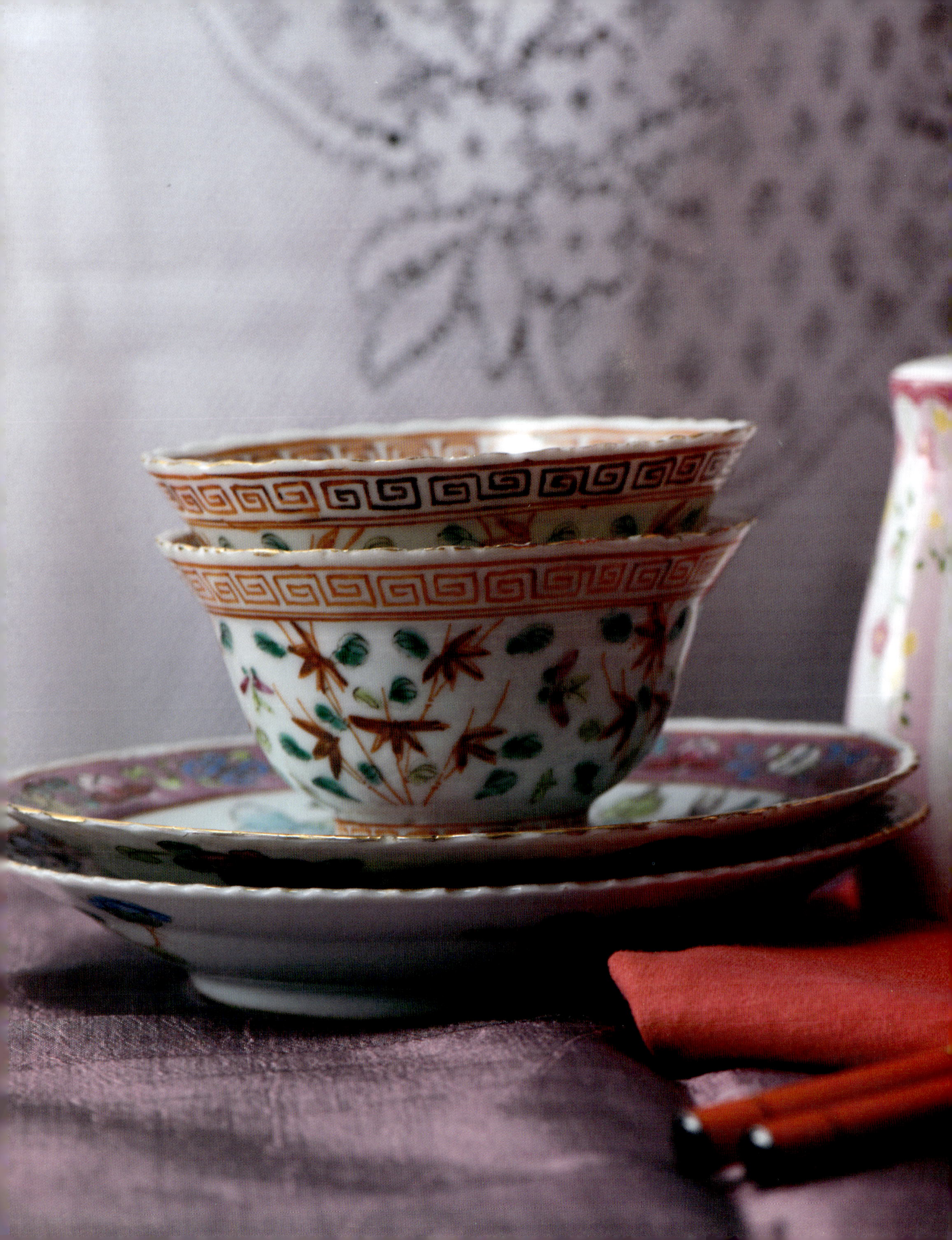

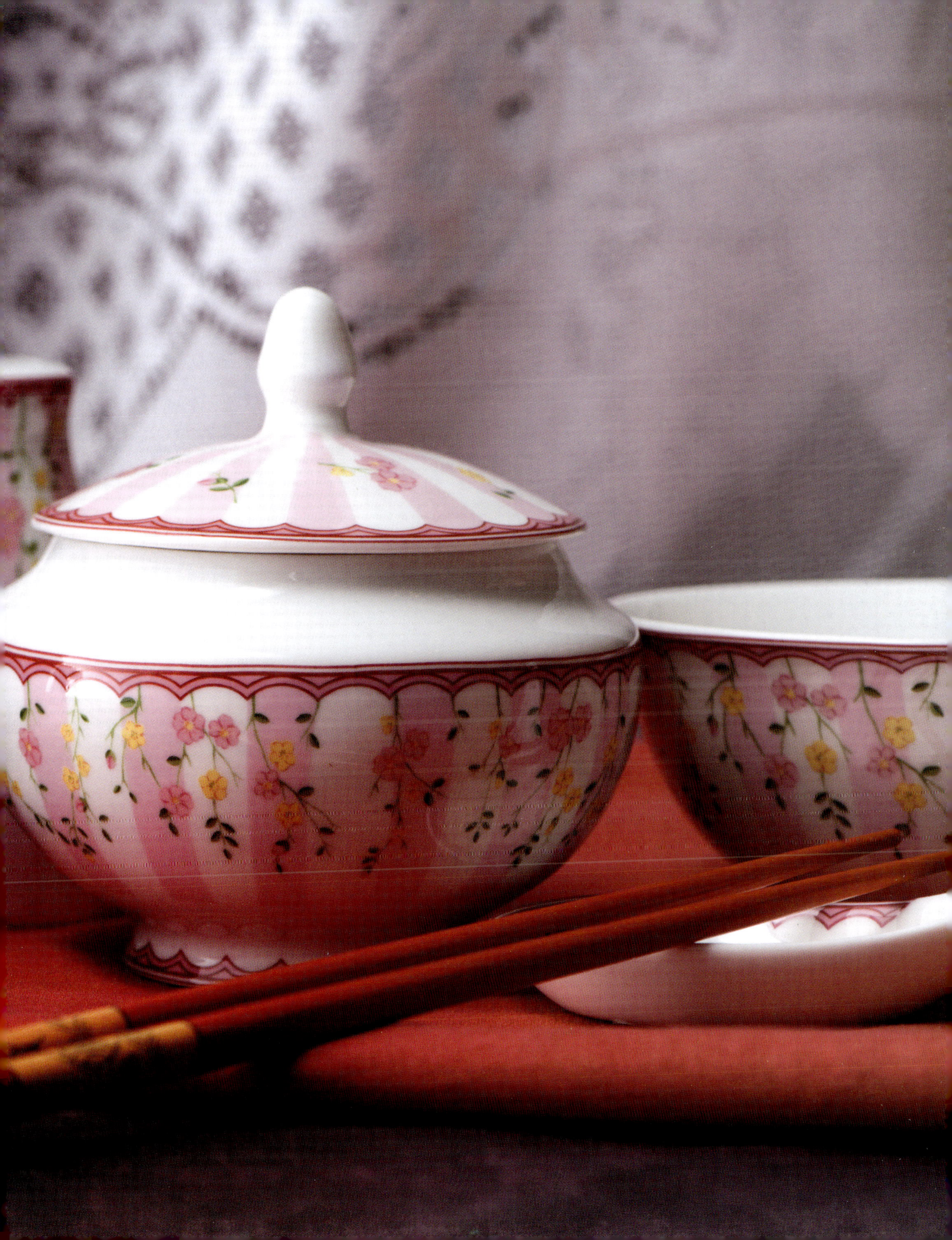

Basic Recipes

Makes 300 g (10 1/2 oz)

Spicy Shrimp Paste (*Sambal Belacan*)

There are different types of spicy shrimp paste. The recipes in this book use spicy shrimp paste that is prepared Malaccan style.

Red chillies 200 g (7 oz)
Toasted shrimp paste (*belacan*) 100 g (3 1/2 oz)

1. Finely blend or grind ingredients together to the desired texture.
2. Freeze unused portion for up to 2–3 months.

Makes 40 g (1 1/3 oz)

Shallot Crisps

Shallots 15, about 150 g (5 1/3 oz), peeled and thinly sliced
Cooking oil 125 ml (4 fl oz / 1/2 cup)

1. Heat cooking oil in a wok over high heat.
2. Fry onions for 2 minutes.
3. Lower heat to medium and fry for another 5 minutes until golden brown.
4. Remove from heat and drain off oil on paper towel.
5. When cooled, store in an airtight container.

Makes 750 ml (24 fl oz / 3 cups)

Chicken Stock

Chicken bones from 2 chickens
Water 1 litre (32 fl oz / 4 cups)

1. Bring chicken bones and water to a boil.
2. Simmer for 1 hour until the liquid reduces to 750 ml (24 fl oz / 3 cups).
3. Strain and set aside to cool. Chicken stock can be refrigerated for a few days.

Makes 120 ml (3$^{3}/_{4}$ fl oz)

Blue Food Colouring–Blue Pea Flower (*Bunga Telang*) Juice

Fresh blue pea flowers (*bunga telang*) 40 g (1$^{1}/_{3}$ oz), washed, stalks and sepals removed
Water 150 ml (5 fl oz)

1. Combine blue pea flowers and water in a saucepan. Bring to a boil.
2. Lower heat and simmer for 3 minutes.
3. Remove from heat and set aside to cool.
4. Squeeze flowers and strain liquid.

NOTE
- Try to use fresh flowers as they impart a nice blue colour to foods. Extra juice can be stored in the refrigerator for a few days or kept frozen for up to 1 month.

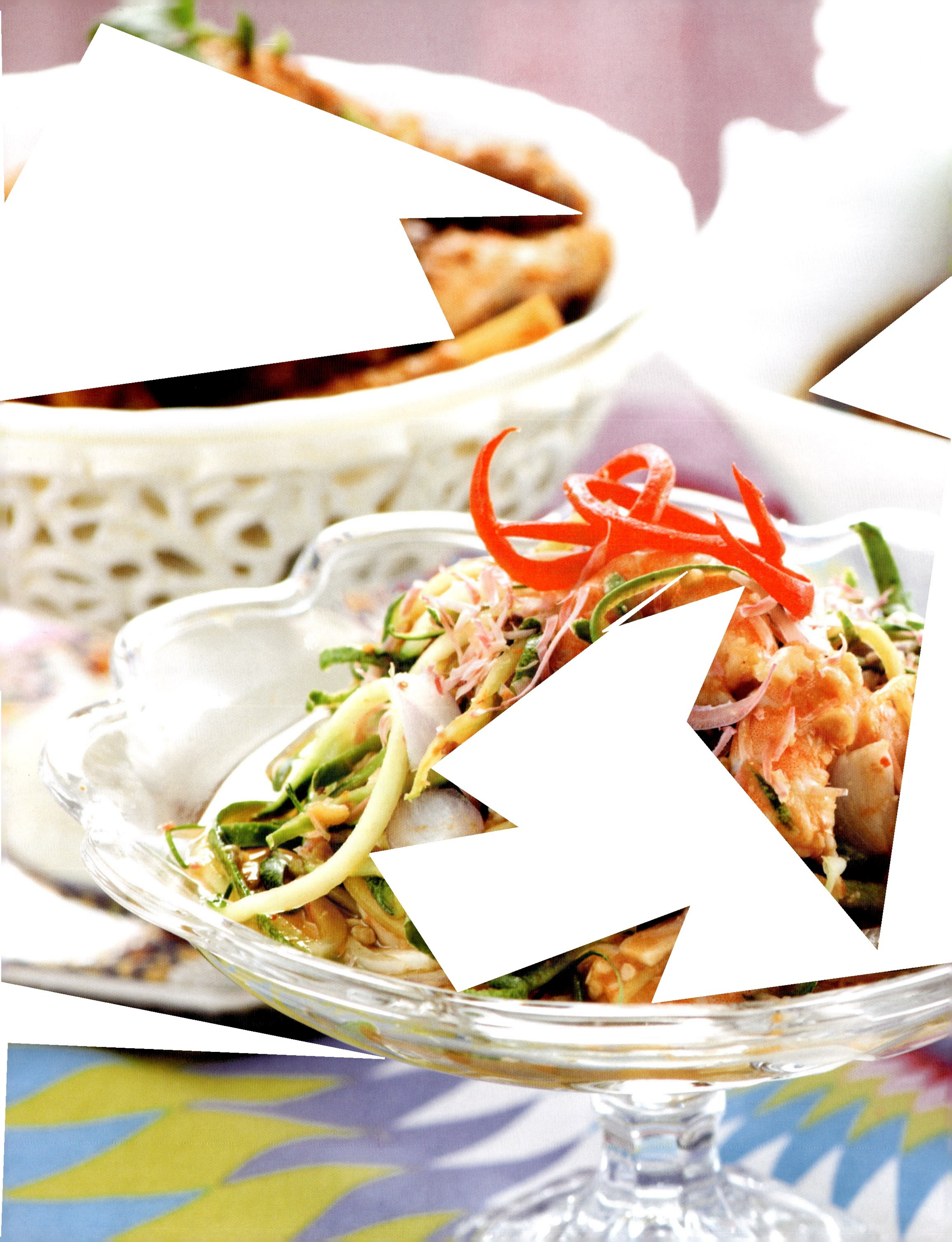

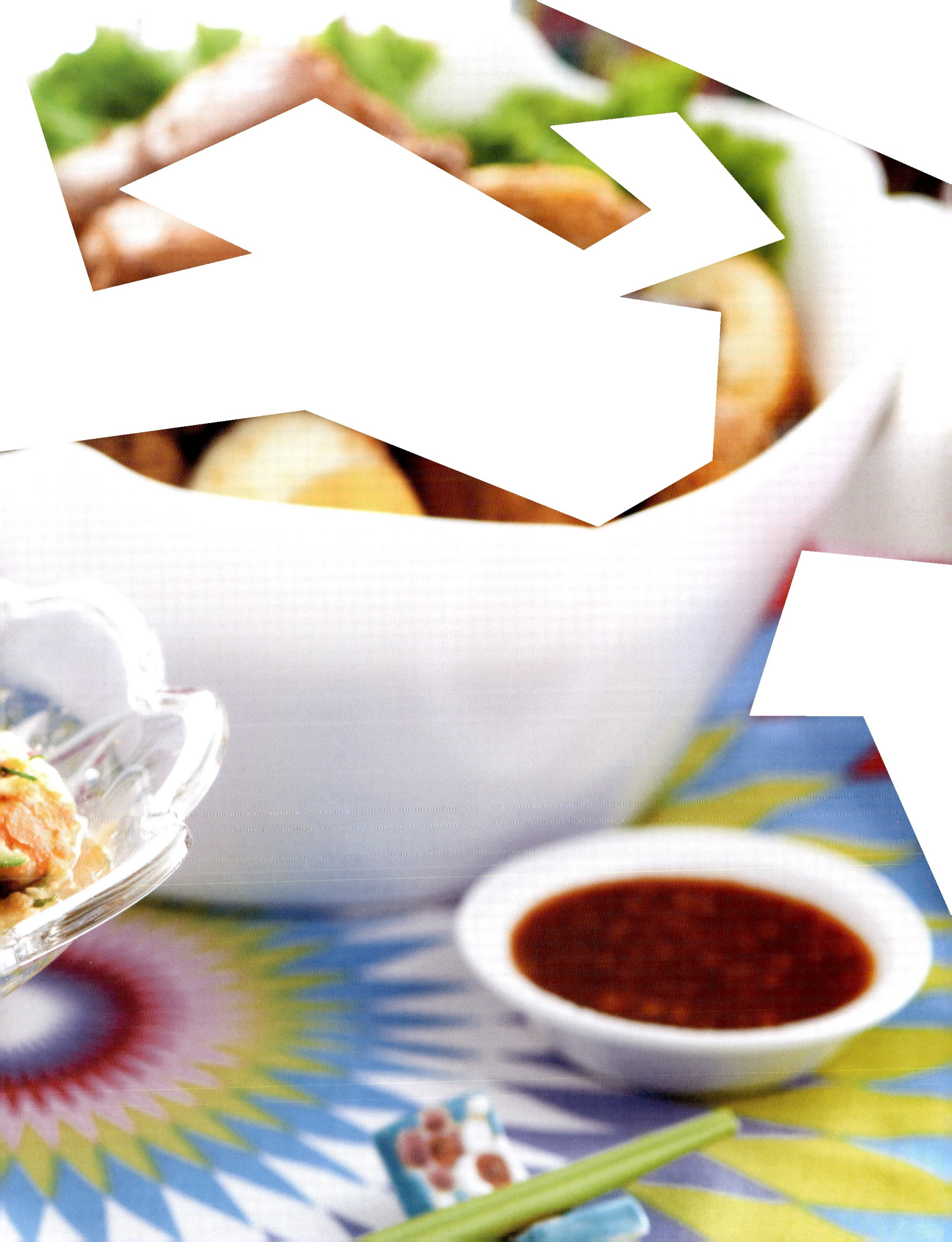

Cooking Tips

Makes 100–150 ml (3 1/3–5 fl oz)

Extracting Coconut Milk from Freshly Grated Coconut

Fresh thick coconut milk can be bought from the wet market or supermarket. You can also extract fresh coconut milk on your own. The amount of coconut milk extracted depends on the amount of strength exerted and the manner in which you extract the milk. All recipes in this book use thick coconut milk that is not diluted with water.

Freshly grated coconut 350 g (12 1/2 oz)

1. Divide grated coconut into smaller portions.
2. Wrap each portion in a muslin cloth and squeeze over a bowl to collect the extracted milk. Do not add water so that the coconut milk is thick.

NOTE
• Squeezing grated coconut in small portions allows you to extract more milk.

For Successful Apam Making

The Nyonyas always cook apam in special traditional brass moulds, which come in various designs, from simple moulds to decorative flower or animal patterns. These moulds are also used to bake the sponge cake, Kuih Baulu.

1. If traditional apam mould is not available, use a small wok and its cover or a non-stick pan.
2. Cook apam over medium heat, subsequently lowering heat halfway through to allow the apam to rise. This prevents burning the base of the apam.
3. Covering the apam helps to cook the top faster, so that the top and bottom of the apam get cooked at the same time. Do not cover apam until bubbles have formed on the surface, otherwise, the apam will have a smooth surface and will not look attractive. If an apam mould cover is unavailable, use an ordinary saucepan cover that fits over the mould. Once the apam is ready, remove from heat and fold into half.
4. Grease mould lightly after each round of baking, and always stir the batter before pouring into the mould. Grease mould when hot to prevent the batter from sticking on it.
5. It is best to use coconut milk extracted from freshly grated coconut without adding any water.

For Successful Talam Making

1. The texture of the cake depends on the type of flour used. Do not mix different brands of flour in a single recipe, as it might affect the texture of the cake. Always test a small portion of batter. Cook in a saucepan and spread it out. Once cooled, gauge the softness and texture of the cooked portion and adjust batter recipe accordingly. Precise measurements are required to make good Nyonya cakes, so it is good practice to test the batter first and take note of the exact measurements of the ingredients.

2. Heat batter until hot. If it becomes lumpy, quickly break up the lumps using a whisk and pour into cake tin.

3. Moisture always collects underneath the lid or cover of the steamer during steaming. Water droplets can spoil the surface of the cake. Dry the cover before closing it over the steamer. If there are water droplets on the cake surface during cooking, gently dab away water with a cloth or tissue paper. Do this every 5 minutes until the cake has set.

4. Water also prevents layers of a cake from sticking together. This is important when preparing layered cakes. Always make sure the surface is dry before topping with another layer of batter. It is also helpful to lightly scratch the surface of the topmost layer with a fork before adding another layer.

5. Have boiling water on hand to replenish water for steaming.

6. Adjust steaming time accordingly. Cake is done when it is opaque.

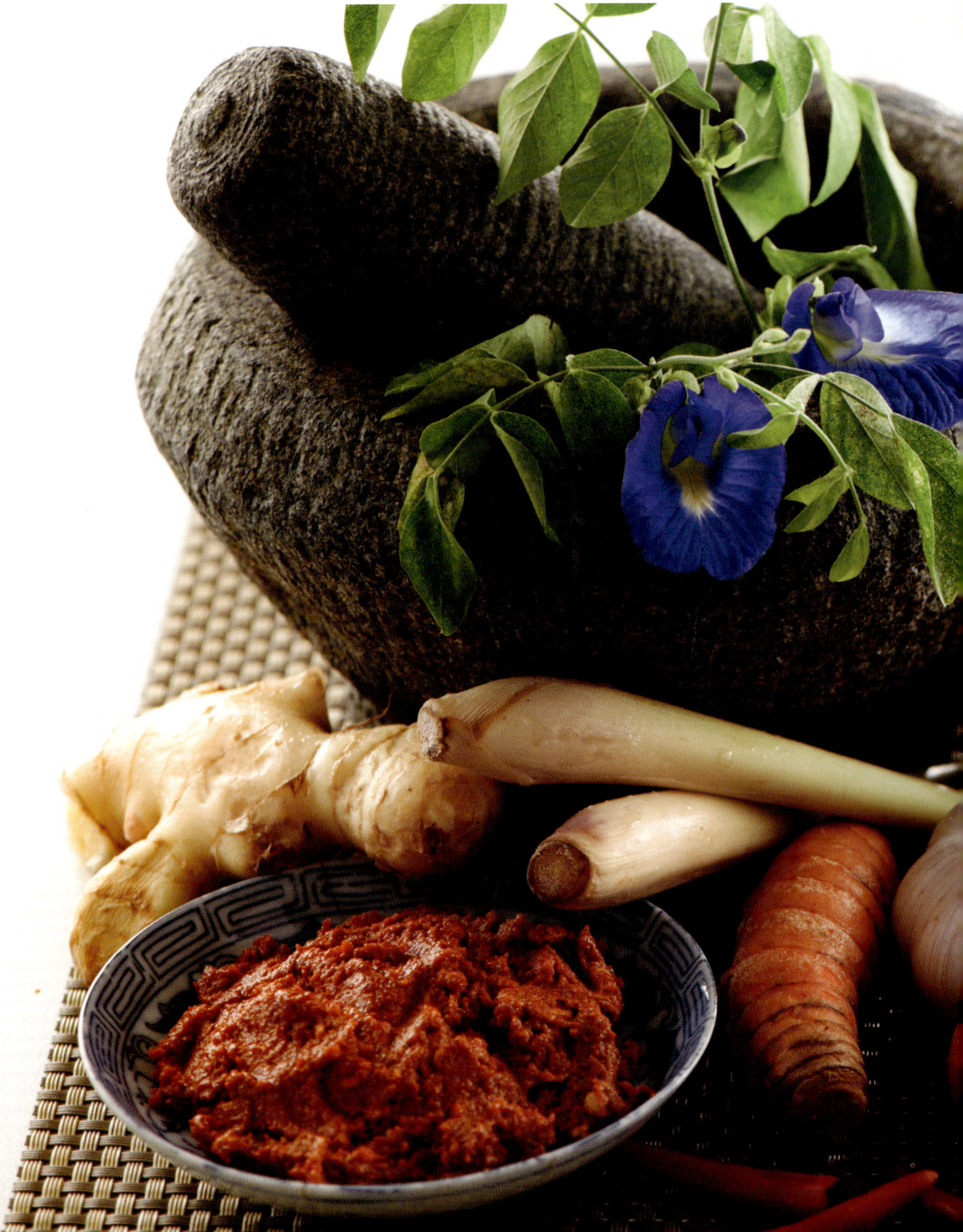

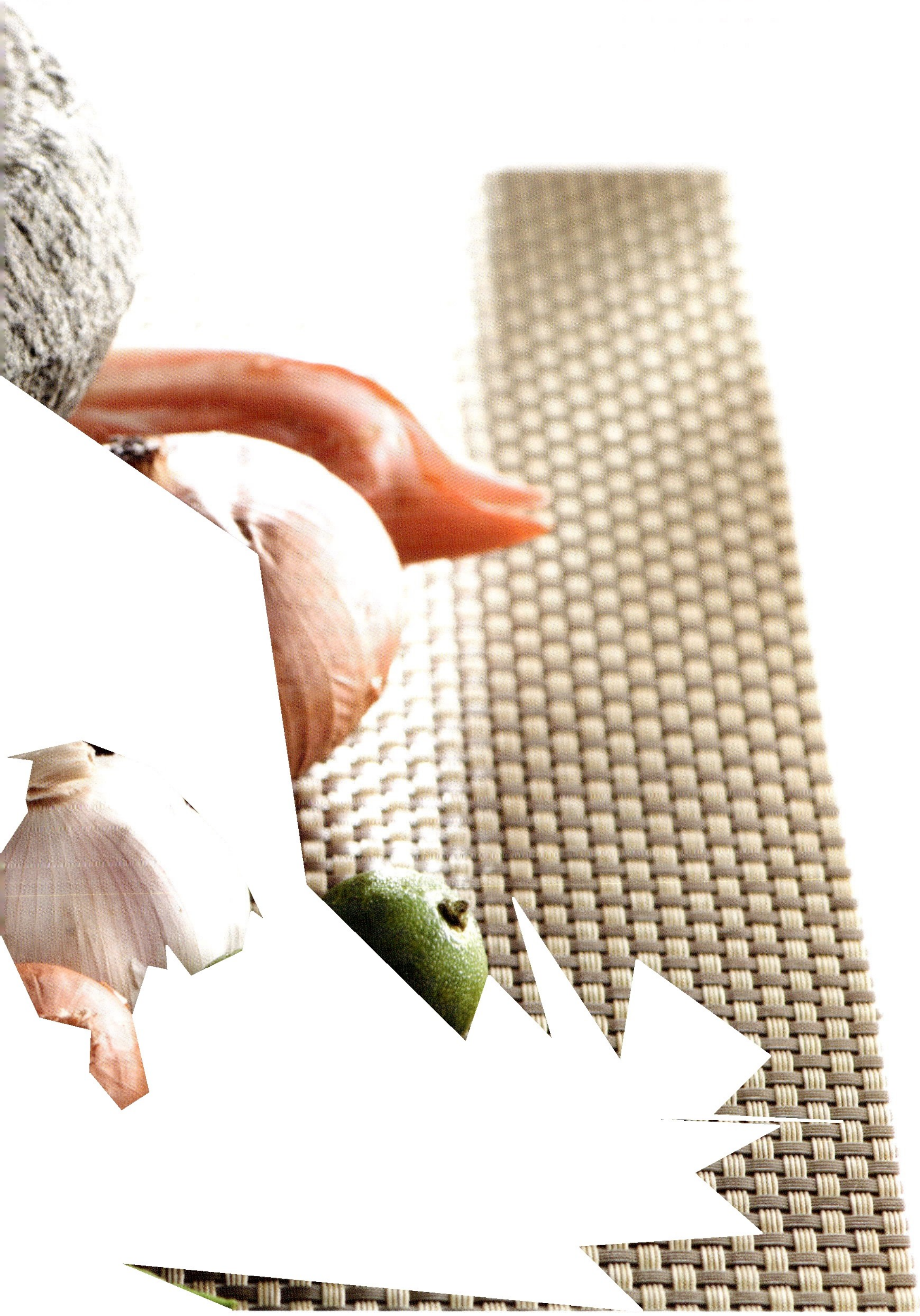

Glossary

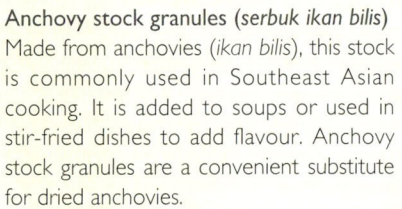

Anchovy stock granules (*serbuk ikan bilis*)
Made from anchovies (*ikan bilis*), this stock is commonly used in Southeast Asian cooking. It is added to soups or used in stir-fried dishes to add flavour. Anchovy stock granules are a convenient substitute for dried anchovies.

Asam Gelugur
The *asam gelugur* fruit tree is native to Peninsular Malaysia. As the fruit is very sour, it is not eaten on its own, but thinly sliced and dried for use in cooking. It is typically used in Peranakan, Malay, Thai and Indonesian cooking. Dried *asam gelugur* slices can be used as a substitute for tamarind pulp.

Banana leaves
These are the fresh cut leaves of the banana plant and a Malay contribution to Peranakan cooking. Banana leaves are used as food wrappers to impart their subtle fragrance to food. To make the leaf more pliable and less prone to tearing, heat it over an open flame or scald with boiling water until it takes on a darker green colour. Clean by wiping with a damp cloth before using.

Bean curd
There are different kinds of bean curd used in the Asian kitchen. Smooth and silky bean curd (tofu) may be eaten cold or hot. Firm bean curd (*tau kwa*) is coarser and has a crumbly texture. Fried bean curd puffs (*tau pok*) are round or square, with a chewy texture and hollow interior. Dried bean curd sticks (*fu chok*), are made from the soy protein skimmed off from boiling soy milk. They impart flavour and texture to dishes they are used in. Pre-fried bean curd sticks are available in supermarkets and grocery stores.

Florence Tan's Best Nyonya Recipes

Bean curd, fermented, red (*nam yee*)
This fermented bean curd is coloured with red yeast rice. It has a strong flavour and should be used sparingly.

Black glutinous rice
Also known as black sticky rice or *pulut hitam*, this rice is purplish rather than black. It has a distinct nutty flavour and is commonly used in desserts.

Blue pea flower (*bunga telang*)
Also known as Butterfly Pea, this small, deep-blue flower gives the blue colouring to snacks and desserts. To extract the juice, boil a handful of flowers with water, then squeeze and strain the liquid. Add a few drops of lime juice, vinegar or a small slice of asam gelugur to enhance the colour.

Candlenut (*buah keras*)
This hard waxy nut has a slightly bitter taste. It also has a nutty texture and flavour. Small quantities are pounded or blended to a paste and used to thicken curry dishes. Candlenuts tend to become rancid very quickly because of their high oil content. To prolong their shelf life, store them in an airtight container in the refrigerator.

Chillies
Chillies come from the capsicum family. Pictured here are fresh finger-length chillies, which are green when unripe and turn red when they ripen. Fresh finger-length chillies are moderately hot, but the red variety is hotter than the green one. There is a slight difference in flavour between the green and red chillies, so it is important to use the type of chilli specified in a recipe. Fresh red chillies may be used whole in cooking or cut in various ways for garnishing. If red chillies are unavailable, substitute 150 g (5 1/3 oz) red chillies for 2 tsp powdered red chilli. Dried chillies, like fresh chillies, are commonly pounded into a paste and used for flavouring or seasoning. Bird's eye chillies, or *cili padi*, are smaller in size. They measure about 4 cm (1 3/4 in) and are very hot.

Glossary 121

Cinnamon
This is a type of spice obtained from the inner bark of cinnamon trees. It is available in powder, or in the form of sticks, which are actually rolled up sheets of cinnamon. Cinnamon is a prominent ingredient in Southeast Asian cuisine, and can be used in meat dishes or snacks and desserts.

Cloves
Cloves are one of the spices added to spice blends such as the five-spice powder and curry powder. As they have a strong and distinctive flavour, it is best to use sparingly or to follow the recommended quantity in a recipe.

Cloud ear fungus (*wan yee*)
Also known as black fungus, the cloud ear fungus comes in dried clusters. They expand when soaked, and add a crunchy texture to the dish.

Coconut milk
This creamy-white milk imparts a rich flavour to many Nyonya dishes. Coconut milk is best extracted from freshly grated coconut flesh. It is best not to add water to freshly extracted coconut milk so that its rich and smooth texture is retained.

Coriander (cilantro) leaves
Also known as Chinese parsley, coriander leaves have a strong fragrance, and can be used as an ingredient in dishes or as a garnish.

Curry leaves
These are essential in curries and they add aroma to many other spicy Nyonya dishes. It is best to use fresh curry leaves, but if these are unavailable, dried curry leaves may be used.

Five-spice powder
This is an aromatic spice blend of cinnamon, star anise, fennel, Sichuan pepper and cloves, which are ground together in varying amounts. It can be used to add flavour to a variety of dishes, and is sold in bottles in supermarkets.

Galangal
This large rhizome (*lengkuas*) is pale pink when young and is more tender and flavourful than the mature one, which is beige in colour. Galangal belongs to the ginger family but cannot be used as a substitute for the common ginger, as its pungency and tang are distinctively different. As it is quite fibrous, cut it into small pieces before pounding or grinding it. If not available, it may be omitted or substituted with lemon grass. Alternatively, use 1/4 tsp powdered galangal in place of 25 g (1 oz) fresh galangal.

Kaffir lime leaves
These leaves are from the kaffir lime plant, and are commonly used fresh or dried in curries for a slightly delicate lemony flavour. Sometimes, they are finely shredded and added to salads or cooked food. If unavailable, the tender new leaves of the lemon or grapefruit plant may be used instead.

Kasturi limes
Also known as kalamansi limes, these citrus fruits produce a juice that is slightly tart. The juice is commonly added to Nyonya dishes for added flavour.

Glossary 123

Lemon grass
This is a fragrant herb with long flat leaves and a bulbous base. Discard the leaves and peel away the tough outer layers of the stem. Use only the lower portion, about 10 cm (4-in) from the root, up to where the purple shade ends. Bruise the bulbous end before adding to gravies and curries for a distinctive lemony flavour. It can also be sliced and finely ground to add flavour in pastes and gravies. If unavailable, use 2 or 3 pieces of thin lemon rind. Alternatively, use 1/2 tsp powdered lemon grass in place of 2 stalks of fresh lemon grass.

Lily buds, dried (*kim chiam*)
These dried flower buds are golden yellow in colour. Soak in water to soften before use, then trim off the hard stem tips. Dried lily buds are usually shredded or knotted before cooking.

Longans, dried
These are made from drying the fresh longan fruits, whose translucent flesh turns dark brown when dried. In Nyonya dishes, dried longans are commonly used to add sweetness to desserts.

Palm sugar (*gula melaka*)
Available in dark brown cylindrical blocks, palm sugar has a slight caramel flavour that can be substituted with brown sugar or maple syrup. Grate or chop into smaller pieces to reduce cooking time.

Polygonum (*kesum*) leaves
These narrow pointed leaves are also known as Vietnamese mint. They are used for garnishing and flavouring curries. The leaves are either crushed or sliced to release their fragrance into the dishes they are added to. They are also added to fish dishes to mask the fishy taste and smell.

124 *Florence Tan's Best Nyonya Recipes*

Prawns (shrimps), dried
These small sun-dried saltwater prawns are available in Asian supermarkets. Best stored refrigerated to retain their freshness. Rinse and soak the required amount in water for 10–15 minutes to soften and remove excess salt before use.

Prawn (shrimp) paste (*belacan*)
This condiment is made from small prawns that have been sun-dried, and then pounded or ground with other spices and seasonings to make a spice mix that forms the base for sambal dishes, curries and spicy gravies. It has a pungent flavour and is widely used in Malay and Nyonya cooking. If unavailable, prawn (shrimp) paste granules can be used instead.

Prawns (shrimps), fermented (*cencaluk*)
This relish is made from small, fine shrimps with long feelers. Hot boiled rice and salt are added to the shrimps, followed by brandy, which aids the fermentation process. The mixture takes 2 to 3 days to mature, after which it is bottled and sold. Before serving as a dip, freshly sliced shallots, chillies and lime juice are added for flavour.

Preserved cabbage (*tung chye*)
These add flavour and crunch to meat, vegetable or soup dishes. They are salty and should be used sparingly.

Preserved soy bean paste (*tau cheo*)
Preserved soy bean paste is a common seasoning that is derived from blending preserved soy beans. Sometimes, chilli is added to make it a hot and spicy condiment. It can be used to thicken the gravy of various dishes.

Rock sugar
Rock sugar is available in Asian supermarkets. It has a rich and delicate flavour compared to regular granulated sugar. Rock sugar can be used in Asian desserts as well as in gravies and sauces for main dishes.

Glossary 125

Round yeast (ragi)
This is a leavening agent containing yeast cells, and is used to raise the dough in making bread and for fermenting beer or whiskey.

Screwpine (pandan) leaves
This long, dark green, blade-like leaf is very fragrant and remarkably versatile. It is added whole to give a distinctive flavour and aroma to savoury dishes, or pounded to extract its juice to lend colour and flavour to desserts and cakes.

Star anise
Star anise, star aniseed, or Chinese star anise, is a spice obtained from the star-shaped pericarp of Illicium verum, a small native evergreen tree of northeast Vietnam and southwest China. It is harvested just before ripening. Star anise enhances the flavour of meat, and is an ingredient of the five-spice powder.

Tamarind pulp
This is extracted from the pods of the tamarind tree, and is commonly used as a souring agent in cooking. It is sold still in their pods or packed into blocks. To use, the pulp must first be mixed with water, and then the liquid strained to remove seeds and fibre. seeds and fibre.

Torch ginger bud (bunga kantan)
Torch ginger bud has a delicate aroma. For cooking, the bud is picked while the petals are still tightly folded. Its intriguing fragrance lends a refreshing aroma to curries and fish dishes. The bud may be eaten raw, where it is finely sliced and added to vegetable salads such as *kerabu* or *rojak*. The fully-bloomed flower is added to soups and gravies to impart its unique flavour.

Turmeric
This rhizome is available fresh or in powdered form. It is bright orange-yellow with a pepper-like bitter taste. It is used in small quantities as a food colouring, a spice and as seasoning for fish or chicken dishes and coconut milk-based gravies. Fresh turmeric leaf is also used to flavour fish and meat dishes. Substitute 1 Tbsp chopped fresh turmeric with 1/4 tsp powdered turmeric.

Weights & Measures

Quantities for this book are given in Metric, Imperial and American (spoon and cup) measures. Standard spoon and cup measurements used are: 1 tsp = 5 ml, 1 Tbsp = 15 ml, 1 cup = 250 ml. All measures are level unless otherwise stated.

LIQUID AND VOLUME MEASURES

Metric	Imperial	American
5 ml	1/6 fl oz	1 teaspoon
10 ml	1/3 fl oz	1 dessertspoon
15 ml	1/2 fl oz	1 tablespoon
60 ml	2 fl oz	1/4 cup (4 tablespoons)
85 ml	2 1/2 fl oz	1/3 cup
90 ml	3 fl oz	3/8 cup (6 tablespoons)
125 ml	4 fl oz	1/2 cup
180 ml	6 fl oz	3/4 cup
250 ml	8 fl oz	1 cup
300 ml	10 fl oz (1/2 pint)	1 1/4 cups
375 ml	12 fl oz	1 1/2 cups
435 ml	14 fl oz	1 3/4 cups
500 ml	16 fl oz	2 cups
625 ml	20 fl oz (1 pint)	2 1/2 cups
750 ml	24 fl oz (1 1/5 pints)	3 cups
1 litre	32 fl oz (1 3/5 pints)	4 cups
1.25 litres	40 fl oz (2 pints)	5 cups
1.5 litres	48 fl oz (2 2/5 pints)	6 cups
2.5 litres	80 fl oz (4 pints)	10 cups

DRY MEASURES

Metric	Imperial
30 grams	1 ounce
45 grams	1 1/2 ounces
55 grams	2 ounces
70 grams	2 1/2 ounces
85 grams	3 ounces
100 grams	3 1/2 ounces
110 grams	4 ounces
125 grams	4 1/2 ounces
140 grams	5 ounces
280 grams	10 ounces
450 grams	16 ounces (1 pound)
500 grams	1 pound, 1 1/2 ounces
700 grams	1 1/2 pounds
800 grams	1 3/4 pounds
1 kilogram	2 pounds, 3 ounces
1.5 kilograms	3 pounds, 4 1/2 ounces
2 kilograms	4 pounds, 6 ounces

OVEN TEMPERATURE

	°C	°F	Gas Regulo
Very slow	120	250	1
Slow	150	300	2
Moderately slow	160	325	3
Moderate	180	350	4
Moderately hot	190/200	370/400	5/6
Hot	210/220	410/440	6/7
Very hot	230	450	8
Super hot	250/290	475/550	9/10

LENGTH

Metric	Imperial
0.5 cm	1/4 inch
1 cm	1/2 inch
1.5 cm	3/4 inch
2.5 cm	1 inch

The publisher wishes to thank Living Quarters Sdn Bhd, Parkson Corporation Sdn Bhd and Luminarc for the loan of tableware used in this book.

Project coordinator	: Christine Chong
Chef	: Florence Tan
Editors	: Audrey Yow (English edition) and Norhafizah Mohamed Yussof (Malay edition)
Designer	: Adithi Khandadi
Photographer	: Pacino Wong of You Studio (All photographs by Pacino Wong of You Studio except the following: Chillies on page 121 and torch ginger bud on page 126 by Hongde Photography; Galangal on page 123 and lemon grass on page 124 by Jambu Studio)
Food stylist	: Anne Rozario
Introduction	: Evelyn Wan
Translator	: Norzailina Nordin
Food preparation	: Patricia Lee, Koh Swee Lian, Koh Kim Lian, Amy Koh
Typing of recipes	: Marianne Chuah

Copyright © 2012 Marshall Cavendish International (Asia) Private Limited

Published by Marshall Cavendish Cuisine
An imprint of Marshall Cavendish International

All rights reserved

No part of this publication may be reproduced, stored in a retrieval system or transmitted, in any form or by any means, electronic, mechanical, photocopying, recording or otherwise, without the prior permission of the copyright owner. Request for permission should be addressed to the Publisher, Marshall Cavendish International (Asia) Private Limited, 1 New Industrial Road, Singapore 536196. Tel: (65) 6213 9300 Fax: (65) 6285 4871 E-mail: genref@sg.marshallcavendish.com Online bookstore: http://www.marshallcavendish.com

Limits of Liability/Disclaimer of Warranty: The Author and Publisher of this book have used their best efforts in preparing this book. The Publisher makes no representation or warranties with respect to the contents of this book and is not responsible for the outcome of any recipe in this book. While the Publisher has reviewed each recipe carefully, the reader may not always achieve the results desired due to variations in ingredients, cooking temperatures and individual cooking abilities. The Publisher shall in no event be liable for any loss of profit or any other commercial damage, including but not limited to special, incidental, consequential, or other damages.

Other Marshall Cavendish Offices:
Marshall Cavendish Corporation, 99 White Plains Road, Tarrytown NY 10591-9001, USA • Marshall Cavendish International (Thailand) Co Ltd. 253 Asoke, 12th Flr, Sukhumvit 21 Road, Klongtoey Nua, Wattana, Bangkok 10110, Thailand • Marshall Cavendish (Malaysia) Sdn Bhd, Times Subang, Lot 46, Subang Hi-Tech Industrial Park, Batu Tiga, 40000 Shah Alam, Selangor Darul Ehsan, Malaysia.

Marshall Cavendish is a trademark of Times Publishing Limited

National Library Board, Singapore Cataloguing-in-Publication Data

Tan, Florence.
Florence's best Nyonya recipes / Florence Tan. – Singapore : Marshall Cavendish Cuisine, c2012.
p. cm.
ISBN : 978-981-4398-20-6
1. Cooking, Peranakan. I. Title.

TX724.5
641.59595 -- dc23   OCN795696550

Printed in Malaysia by Times Offset (M) Sdn Bhd